ÆNGLA LAND
State-building and Nation-Forging in Anglo-Saxon England

Published by Peripeteia Press

First published October 2015

ISBN: 978-0-993077869

Peripeteia.webs.com

About the authors

Originally from Cheshire, **Chris Eldridge** read History at Magdalene College, Cambridge. After a stint in the nuclear industry, he joined the teaching profession in 2003. He is currently Head of History at Wells Cathedral School, where he also runs the Polydorian Project, an initiative championing the study of medieval history in British schools: polydorian.wells-cathedral-school.com.

Chris lives in the cathedral city of Wells, Somerset with his family. This is his first book.

An experienced Head of English and freelance writer, **Neil Bowen** has been teaching English for nearly twenty years and is the author of many articles and resources for a range of publishers. Neil has a Masters Degree in Literature & Education from Cambridge University and he is a member of Ofqual's experts panel for English. For peripeteia press, Neil has written 'The Art of Writing English Essays' for GCSE and he is the co-author or 'The Art of Writing English Essays' for A-level and beyond.

To Nicky, Katherine and my own Alfred the Great with love.

Contents

Note on sources

The multiple translations of Anglo-Saxon documents available can lead to confusion. To maximise transparency, wherever possible, those within the comprehensive *English Historical Documents* Volume 1 edited by Dorothy Whitelock (London, 1979) are therefore used. The principle exception are those covering the reign of Alfred the Great, where Simon Lapidge and Michael Keynes' more modern translation of Asser's *Life of Alfred* and supporting documents are utilised (London, 2004).

List of maps and diagrams

Introduction

The 550 years between the fall of the Roman Empire and the Norman Conquest is the most neglected period in English history. Traditionally it has been written off as 'the Dark Ages', a time of violence and barbarism between the glories of Ancient Rome and the Norman civilisation. Traditionally it has been viewed as a period of which little is known and little can be learned.

Certainly less written evidence survives from the era than any other time in English history and there are comparatively few physical remains either. An historian studying the rise of London, for instance, will look in vain for pre-Conquest buildings. Apart from a few stretches of Roman wall, the late 11th century Tower of London is the oldest intact building above ground. Partly this is the result of 'Dark Age' culture – its British, Anglo-Saxon and Viking inhabitants were largely illiterate and usually built in perishable wood, not enduring stone. But primarily it is the result of the systematic obliteration of the remains of the period carried out by its successors. The Normans demolished and rebuilt all but 50 Anglo-Saxon churches, including every single cathedral as part of a deliberate policy of cultural domination over their conquered Anglo-Saxon subjects. Less deliberate, but just as devastating was the destruction of records from the period that occurred in the 16th century when Henry VIII destroyed the monastic libraries.

As a result it is tempting to see 1066 as a 'year zero' moment when meaningful English history begins, certainly that is how history has traditionally been taught in British secondary schools. To do so however, deprives us of some of the most vibrant periods and personalities in England's historical tapestry – England's nation forger Alfred the Great, her most ambitious builder Offa of Mercia, her first queen, Aethelflaed, as well as her first historian Bede to name but a few. It is also historically just plain wrong to see 1066 as the moment English history begins.

The idea of England first appears courtesy of Alfred the Great in 878, everything that follows afterwards is evolution, the Normans and their successors simply adding to a template which was firmly established by 900. But if we are to truly understand how the complicated blend of state development, faith and identity that made up the medieval period of English history came into being, we must start earlier, round the year 600 when Northumbria, the first recognisable medieval state emerges out of the tumult that followed the fall of the Roman Empire in Britain nearly two centuries earlier.

This book will therefore follow current historical nomenclature in referring to the period between the fall of Rome and the Norman Conquest as the Early Medieval period rather than the Dark Ages, reflecting the essential continuity in the development of the medieval English state before and after the Conquest. This book is at heart a political history seeking to trace the unique story of how England developed into the world's first nation state in the 9th and the 10th centuries. Such a drastic change cannot be studied entirely in insolation and, where relevant, attention is also given to how culture, society, economics and above all religion fed into this dramatic story.

Chapters 1 and 2 set out the context of our study, tracing events in early medieval Europe and how they impacted upon England and, by briefly assessing the 'Migration Period' of Anglo-Saxon invasion from 410-600, form a backdrop out of which later political developments can be better understood. Chapter 3 forms an overview of the institutions and assumptions behind Anglo-Saxon political structures of government and paints a picture of the mindset of Anglo-Saxon government and how its people responded to it. Thereafter Chapters 4-10 follow a broadly chronological study of the phases in the evolution of the English nation state, tracking development in the leading kingdoms in the 7th-9th centuries – Northumbria, Mercia and Wessex respectively, assessing the impact of the Viking invasions and then considering the creation and evolution of the united state of England in the first century of its existence – the 10th century. Detailed analysis ends at the turn of the first millennium. The last phase of the period, from 1002-1066 returns to a broad view, the justification being that the process of English nation state building was completed by that juncture and that this period was characterised less by political evolution and more by a multi-national successional crisis involving Anglo-Saxon English, Scandinavians and Normans. William the Conqueror's victory in 1066, this book argues, marks the beginning of the end of the crisis and the emergence of a new phase of political development which essentially evolves from the early medieval English state as it existed by 1002. Chapter 11 finishes our study with an overview of historiography of the period for the benefit of students who wish to develop their studies within the wider fabric of early medieval history.

This book is conceived primarily as an introduction to early medieval English history for sixth form students and undergraduates. With this in mind chapters 4-10, covering the detail of the period, begin with a brief chronology of main events and individuals, conclude with an overview of current historiographical arguments and present a series of questions which could form the basis either of essays or discussion derived from the Cambridge Pre-U syllabus for Year 12-13 students (www.cie.org). Terminology has been kept as simple as possible throughout. Where unfamiliar phrases and words have been used they may be found in the glossary at the back of the book.

My intention has been to provide a study which is accessible rather than universal. It is hoped that the book will provide a much needed introductory text to early medieval England, one that can form the basis of further study as well as providing a clear overview of the first, crucial phase of English history to the general reader.

Chris Eldridge
August 2015

Chapter 1: Mimesis – an overview of early medieval Europe

Key events:

451: Council of Chalcedon sees split between Catholic and Orthodox churches emerge

476: Formal end of the Western Roman Empire

507: Clovis, King of the Franks, gains control of most of modern France, founding the first post-Roman Empire in Europe, the Merovingians

527-65: Byzantine Emperor Justinian briefly reunites east and western Europe

543: St Benedict issues the definitive early medieval code for monastic living

597: St Augustine of Canterbury begins conversion of the Anglo-Saxons to Christianity

610: Mohammed founds Islam in Arabia

634: Islamic conquest of the Middle East, Africa and Spain begins

718: Byzantines temporarily halt Islamic expansion in Eastern Europe

737: Charles Martel beats the Moslems at Poitiers halting the Islamic invasion of Western Europe

792: Beginning of Viking raids into Christendom

800: Charlemagne is crowned Holy Roman Emperor, first emperor of Western Europe since the fall of Rome

815: Anglo-Saxon invasion of modern England completed after King Egbert of Wessex conquers the Britons of Cornwall

834: Viking invasion of English kingdoms begins

843: Treaty of Verdun splits Carolingian Empire into French, German and Italian kingdoms

878: Alfred the Great of Wessex defeats Vikings at Edington and begins process of unifying England

900: Alfonso III of Castile begins the 'Reconquista' against the Moslems of Spain

904: Installation of Sergius III makes beginning of 'papal dark age' until 963 when the papacy is controlled by corrupt Theophylacti family

911: Duchy of Normandy established under Rollo the Viking

937: Victory of Athelstan of Wessex over Vikings, Scots and Britons marks formal completion of England as the first European nation state

979: Renewal of Viking attacks on England

1009: Devastation of the Holy Sepulchre by Islamic fundamentalists

1016: Canute absorbs England into the Danish Empire

1025: Byzantine Empire begins to decline

1042: Edward the Confessor regains the English throne for the Cerdicynn dynasty

1046: Holy Roman Emperor Henry III deposes three popes in succession, peak of imperial control over papacy

1053: Normans establish an empire in southern Italy and Sicily

1054: Schism between Catholic and Orthodox churches

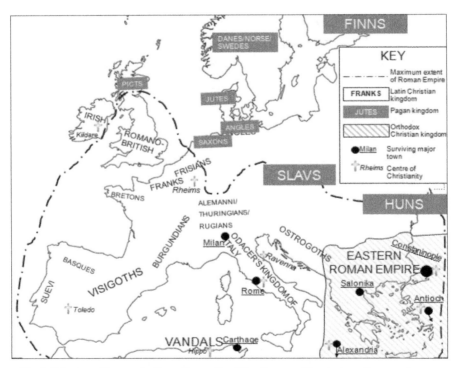

Fig 1: Western Europe in the aftermath of the Roman Empire's collapse, circa 476 AD

Surviving the apocalypse

The Sack of Rome 410 AD by JN Sylvestre (1890)

Medieval Europe began with the collapse of the Roman Empire in the west. This was a long drawn out process with its roots as far back as the 3rd century AD, but the process was formally completed in 476 when the last Emperor Romulus Augustulus was overthrown by Odoacer, King of the Germanic tribes, who had seized control of Italy. Odoacer and his fellow Germanic leaders divided the central provinces of the former Western Empire into tribal kingdoms, leaving the outlying regions, such as Britain, isolated and vulnerable in turn to their own invasions. Civil war was rife; trade routes collapsed, agriculture declined and as a consequence the urban centres that defined western Europe plummeted in size – Rome's population fell from a million at the start of the 3rd century to approximately 30,000 three hundred years later. Inevitably the Romano-Greek system of education crumbled as well as even the most basic notions of government and justice.

The Roman tradition of prophesy had left a legacy of visions of how the world would end. Many inhabitants of this post-classical world, living as they did amidst the ruins of a more sophisticated past, understandably believed that this end time was imminent:

"When the empire of the Romans shall have ceased, then Antichrist will be clearly revealed and he will sit in the house of the Lord in Jerusalem...Then there will be a great persecution, the likes of which never happened before of since. But the Lord will shorten those days on account of the elect and Antichrist will be killed by the power of the Lord, by the archangel Michael in the Mount of Olives."[1]

In reality, the collapse of Roman civilisation was not as complete as it might appear. The Eastern Roman Empire, centred on Constantinople survived preserving structures, traditions and memories of classical learning which it would in time transfuse back into the west. Moreover Western Europe never truly lapsed into anarchy; its new rulers were pragmatists who recognised the inherent strength of Roman institutions of governance and in many cases preserved them – the noble families of the Roman senate, for example, continued to hold office within the government of Odoacer and his successors as *praefecti* in charge of provinces identical to their Roman predecessors.

The Church of the Holy Wisdom (Hagia Sophia), Istanbul. Under construction in the midst of Roman collapse in the west, it represents the continuity of the Roman *imperium* in the east.

Beyond simple pragmatism on the part of the Germanic kings, the main

---
[1] *The Prophecy of the Tiburtine Sibyl* c. 380 AD

reason for this continuity was the persistence of the Christian faith as a unifying force across Europe. By the time of the formal collapse of the western Empire, the Germanic kings were largely Christian and made extensive use of the Roman Church with its literate and administratively skilled clergy and emphasis on obedience to hierarchy. To a considerable extent, The Pope successfully replaced the Emperor as a universal force of authority in Western Europe. A second date for the beginning of the medieval period in Western Europe is therefore the Council of Chalcedon. Held in 451 it comprised a gathering of senior clergy from across Europe, out of which a sharp divergence opened up between the beliefs and structure of the Orthodox Christian tradition, rooted in the surviving eastern provinces of the Roman Empire, and those of the Catholic tradition based in Rome and the successor kingdoms to the western Empire.

This divide between a Greek-speaking east and a Latin-speaking west split Europe religiously and politically, culminating in the formal schism of the European Church in 1054. The Eastern Roman metamorphosised into the Byzantine Empire in the 7th century through an overhaul of its government and traditions that owed more to contemporary Greek and Persian ideas than it did to classical ones. This division into east and west was a defining feature of medieval history; in the west the consequence was that from the 7th century a rapid process of political change began, fuelled by dialogue between two traditions:

- a secular, Germanic tradition of tribal kingship common to most of the royal dynasties of early medieval Europe
- the traditions of governance and belief of the Catholic Church, rooted in classical notions of philosophy and hierarchy.

In different forms this dialogue between church and state would dominate western European politics until the Reformation of the 16th and 17th centuries.

In the short term the inevitable tension between Germanic and Catholic ideas led to permanent turbulence in the shape and relative powers of early medieval states and the Church. As R.W. Southern summarises, even in the tenth century, 500 years after the fall of the Western Roman Empire, these tensions remained unresolved:

'Over a great part of Europe there was no regime which promised a settled political order. Behind the facade of strong or weak rulers, there was an incoherent jumble of laws and customs, difficult to adjust to, watch over and hard to understand...barbaric codes of law jostled with varying mixtures of Roman law, local custom and violence, and besides all this there was a maze of Church law through which every bishop had to find his way as best he could'.[2]

The routes out of these tensions lay in theories of governance and society developed by the 9th centuries governments of modern day Germany and England - the former evolved the feudal system which restored social and economic stability, whilst out of the latter developed the institutions of the nation state, the definitive system of European system of government which has since spread throughout the world. Before we consider these revolutions, the beliefs underpinning early medieval western Europe need consideration.

Resignation, *mimesis* and beyond

The modern separation of governance, religion and wider learning is an innovation of the 17th century that would have been incomprehensible to the early medieval mind. The man of learning, whether of the purely classical or Christian tradition was expected to apply himself with equal facility to problems of kingship, man's relationship with God and the maintenance of prosperity in society – in short he was expected to literally know everything[3]. As a result, in the medieval period the same learned individuals habitually ran the Church and government in addition to institutions of learning, sometimes simultaneously. The source of their thinking for all of these activities derived

---

[2] Southern R.W. *The Making of the Middle Ages* (1973) p.17.
[3] Social historian Alan Hodge and literary historian Sir Peter Quennell believed that as late as the 1650s it was possible for an intelligent individual to possess universal knowledge of all branches of western learning – the last person to perform this feat being poet, philosopher and civil servant John Milton (1608-74). Thereafter the pool of human knowledge inexorably broadened prompting 'the age of specialisation'. Hodge A and Quennell P 'When did it become impossible to know everything?' in *History Today* April 1952 Editorial.

from the same origin, namely knowledge as the revealed will of God.

In the early medieval Europe this concept of knowledge underwent an existential crisis. The classical world that had formed the foundation of learning lay in ruins, and the early medieval world which replaced it was violent, shapeless and incoherent. Early medieval Europeans lived in a world of *regression* – their present was clearly inferior to their past in sophistication and understanding. In Western Europe, Roman relics such as roads, aqueducts and even stone buildings were used until they fell apart, after which they could not be replaced. A 21st century equivalent would be the loss of the ability to make the microchip, compelling communications technology to decay and eventually to become extinct.

A 19th century illustration of the Council of Chalcedon of 451 – the moment of schism between east and west Europe.

The roots of the political and cultural split between eastern and western Europe can be explained by their contrasting reactions to this situation. In the east the Roman Empire's institutions survived in a battered and modified form, sufficient for a semblance of classical government and knowledge to survive. Concurrently, eastern Christianity came to the collective belief that God had finished revealing His will to mankind. At the Council of Chalcedon in 451 the Patriarchs of the eastern Church stated the belief that everything which God willed humanity to know could be found in the words of Jesus, the pages of the scriptures and the works of the philosophers of the Church which they called the 'fathers', such as Cyril, Origen and Athanasius. Consequently after 451 eastern Orthodox Christianity and the Byzantine state shaped by it moved into a state of care and maintenance in which existing knowledge was preserved, but little new was added. In essence therefore, Eastern Europe's response to the decay of knowledge was to allow that which remained to atrophy.

Paralysis in the east contrasts with necessary change in the west. The collapse of the status quo of government and knowledge meant that atrophy was impossible; the only two options were either apocalyptic or progressive – eschatology and *mimesis*[4] respectively. Eschatology, the belief in an imminent collapse of the world of mankind, was embraced by a minority who believed they were living in the days foretold by St. John of Patmos in the Book of Revelation, as depicted overleaf in an early fifteenth century image. Eschatology affirmed that the second coming of Jesus was imminent after which the current world would come to a dramatic end:

"And I saw a new heaven and a new earth: for the first heaven and the first earth were passed away; and there was no more sea. And I John saw the holy city, new Jerusalem, coming down from God out of heaven, prepared as a bride adorned for her husband. And I heard a great voice out of heaven saying, Behold, the tabernacle of God is with men, and he will dwell with them, and they shall be his people, and God himself shall be with them, and be their God. And God shall wipe away all tears from their eyes; and there

---

[4] Literally 'Imitation', a Greek term with multiple meanings, in this context it refers to the philosophical view expounded by Plato and Christianised by Augustine of Hippo that the key to human knowledge was to discover and then to imitate the behaviour of God.

shall be no more death, neither sorrow, nor crying, neither shall there be any more pain: for the former things are passed away." [5]

Early medieval philosophers who subscribed to this view, known as Preterists, argued that as the world was doomed, mankind should concentrate its remaining energies on attending to the state of its soul to ensure admission into God's 'new heaven and new earth'. Although such thinking produced a great deal of comfort for individuals living in post classical Europe, it clearly represents a dead end in terms of mankind's knowledge.

A medieval Doom painting – preterists argued that the Last Judgement of mankind was in progress.

Fortunately for western civilisation, a more optimistic school of thought prevailed – *mimesis*. *Mimesis* was the belief that the appropriate response to the current wretched state of mankind was to combine knowledge from the past with an aspiration to attain more knowledge in the future. The purpose of these activities was that man would grow to imitate the omniscient knowledge of God, albeit imperfectly, and in so doing increase in prosperity on earth and attain salvation in heaven. St Augustine of Hippo's hugely ambitious and

---

[5] *The Book of Revelation* Ch. 21 Vs 1-4.

influential *City of God* (completed circa 430 AD) firmly established *mimesis* as the dominant form of early medieval thought in western Europe. This was a work that sought to provide a blueprint for the effective ordering of the whole of society, economics and the state and, to achieve perfection of existence, all mankind had to do was use its intellect to discover God's omniscient purpose and reject its own selfish, self destructive will. What makes *City of God* so vital to the development of western thought and government is that it provides an ingenious means by which a Christian might combine pre-Christian learning with a desire to progress in the future and still conform to the will of God:

'[God] wills that Himself, that which he makes others discover... When the time of the manifestation of anything, which God foreknows will come, is not yet come, we say 'It shall be when God wills it'. It is not that God shall have any other will then He had before, but that discoveries shall be made in accordance with His eternal, unchanging will which had from all eternity ordained.'[6]

In essence, the Christian man can, indeed should, strive for a better world safe in the knowledge that he will only learn what God intends that he should learn.

Three early medieval individuals in particular built on St Augustine's Christian *mimesis* and through it essentially laid the foundation of western medieval scholarship and governance:

1. Boethius, whose lifespan (c.480-524/6) corresponded exactly with the final collapse of the western Roman Empire preserved classical Platonic notions about the meaning of life in his *Consolation of Philosophy.*

2. Cassiodorus (c.485-580) an historian who conserved a huge body of classical knowledge and used it to establish a prototype for medieval universities and monasteries on his own Italian estate known as the *Vivarium.*

3. Gregory the Great (Pope 540-604), a noted theologian whose greatest

---

[6] St Augustine of Hippo *The City of God Book* XXII Ch. II 'Of the eternal and unchangeable will of God'.

contribution was to create a solid framework of Christian government within the Catholic church, preserving Roman notions of hierarchy which would serve as a model of governance across Europe for the next millennia.

Boethius, Cassiodorus and Gregory the Great – saviours of classical learning.

Out of these foundations rose a vibrant tradition of learning within the medieval Catholic Church, educating academics, such as Bede of Northumbria and political clerics who formed the backbone of both secular and religious government, such as Adalard of Corbie, who, as Charlemagne's chief minister at the start of the 9th century, presided over territories as great as the Roman Emperors themselves. Thus, just as civilisation had been formally defined by the borders of the Roman Empire, by the 7th century it was likewise defined by the bounds of Christendom.

Renewed threats

Despite seismic cultural and political change, before the 7th century Christian Europe was surprisingly free of external threats. With the exception of Sassanid Persians in the east, its pagan neighbours were largely too divided to present a sustained threat, and by the start of the 7th century even the Sassanids had been fought to a standstill by the Byzantines beyond the bounds of Europe herself.

The rise of Islam and its whirlwind conquest of most of the Middle East and North Africa from the 630s onwards destroyed this tranquillity. The well organised and united early Islamic caliphates would provide a constant threat to Christendom for the remainder of the medieval period, with two shifting front lines emerging, one in modern Turkey lapping at the borders of the Byzantine Empire and a second in Spain, from which the last Moslem kingdom would not be evicted until 1492.

In the north the last pagan threat to Christendom emerged from the end of the 8th century onwards – Scandinavian raiders, traders and conquerors collectively known as 'Vikings' after the Nordic *Vikingr* or 'wanderer'. Well organised, extremely mobile thanks to their swift and shallow drafted longships and utterly ferocious, Viking warriors were the terror of Europe in the 9th century. Being pagans, they had no respect for Church or clergy. Consequently wealthy and isolated monasteries were often their preferred targets. The *Anglo-Saxon Chronicle* for the year 793 records the first such raid, on the Northumbrian monastery of Lindisfarne wherein 'The harrowing inroads of heathen men made lamentable havoc in the Church of God on Holy Island by rapine and slaughter'[7].

The Viking longship, blight of early medieval Christendom.

Worse was to come. By the 830s raiding had turned to conquest. Soon much of Scotland, Ireland, northern England was overrun and inroads were being made down the continental rivers into modern Germany, Poland and Russia.

---

[7] *The Anglo-Saxon Chronicle* entry for the year 793 in Ed. Whitelock, D. *English Historical ocuments Volume 1 c. 500–1042.* (1996, London) – henceforth referred to as E.H.D. Vol. 1.

Current historical opinion differs as to whether the Vikings were a totally predatory force, as contemporary sources such as the *Anglo-Saxon Chronicle* would have us believe, or whether their goal was cultural and economic assimilation. Archaeology of the multicultural Viking capital of Jorvik (modern York) supports the latter notion, suggesting a city under loose Viking overlordship in which Northumbrian institutions of church and state appear to have continued to function. Nonetheless the Viking assaults on the monastic foundations that preserved and dissimulated knowledge, such as Jarrow and Monkwearmouth, meant that the precarious survival of European civilisation was once again under threat.

The Vikings were, in the short term, contained by military reform within Christendom. By the end of the 7th century their advance had stalled owing to the establishment of a network of fortified towns and the conscription of a substantial militia to man them, as well as standing navies by the Wessex monarchy in England and the Franks and Holy Roman Empire on the continent. Longer term, the Viking homeland would be assimilated into Christendom by missionaries, the first despatched by Charlemagne's son, Louis the Pious, in 826. By 935 with the accession of the Christian Harold Bluetooth as king of Denmark, the Viking homeland was structurally, if not entirely, Christian. However Viking conquests did not cease; indeed England was once again subject to raiding in the 990s. These attacks no longer posed a threat to European civilisation though, as the Christianised Vikings focussed their incursions on towns and fortifications as opposed to monasteries. Indeed Christian Viking dynasties, such as the House of Cnut in England and Rollo in Normandy, regarded themselves as stout defenders of the Christian faith and became patrons of Christian knowledge themselves – the Norman abbey of Bec, founded in 1034, for example, would evolve into the foremost centre of Christian government in northern Europe in the 11th century.

The greatest consequences of the Moslem and Viking threats to Christendom lies in the changes in society and government they stimulated. The 8th and 9th centuries may have been a time of crisis in western Europe, but as is so often the case, crisis also proved to be a driver of dynamic change. Two individuals in particular had a transformative influence: Charlemagne and Alfred the Great.

The Carolingian and Alfredian Legacies

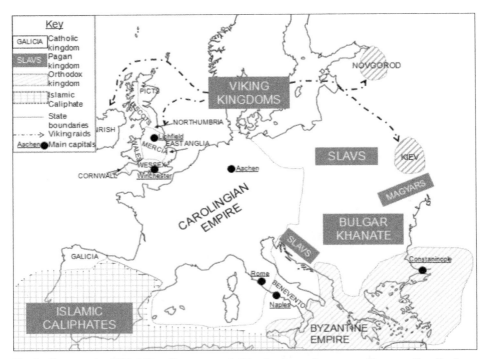

Fig.2: Europe in 800 AD – the year of Charlemagne's coronation as the first Holy Roman Emperor.

Charlemagne ('Charles the Great') was originally King of the Franks, inheriting a throne in 768 that his father Pepin had seized in a papal-sponsored coup from the Merovingian dynasty. He gained the support of the papacy by defending it from the aggressive intentions of the Lombards of northern Italy, by pursuing an aggressive campaign of conquest against the pagan Saxons of northern Germany and by pushing into northern Spain to create a cushion against Islamic expansion into western Europe. This military success led to Charlemagne ruling over the first united western European

Empire since the days of Rome. As a token of this he was crowned Holy Roman Emperor by Pope Leo III, a title which would survive until 1805. A united Christendom under the leadership of a pious, God-fearing monarch, the dream of St Augustine, seemed to be becoming a reality.

However for all its size, Charlemagne's empire was never secure. Threatened by rebellious Christian subjects within, Charlemagne had to contend with pagans to the north as well as Moslems to the south. These threats required a large and efficient military machine which in turn required adequate support. Out of these needs came Charlemagne's edict tying ownership of land with a responsibility for military service, a system later known as fiefdom, the basis around which later medieval armies were assembled. His summons of 806 to Fulrad, Abbot of St. Quentin in 808 is symptomatic of those that European rulers would issue for the next 700 years:

14th century bust of Charlemagne.

'Be it known to you that we shall hold our general assembly this year in eastern Saxony... Wherefore we command you to be present there on 17 June with your men well armed and equipped... There should be provisions for three months and weapons and clothing for six.'[8]

To meet such obligations landowners required both stable sources of labour to farm their lands and economic prosperity to sell their surplus. Charlemagne shared the Church's aversion to slavery, but did accept the need for control of the labour market, hence he acknowledged the existence of the class of *manicipia* or 'bondsmen', unfree labourers who were owned by the great estates they worked upon. In its later incarnation of serfdom, bondsmanship would, with fiefdoms, form the twin pillars of the social system which would characterise high medieval Europe – feudalism.

---

[8] Cited in Riche P. *The Carolingians* (University of Pennsylvania Press, 1983) p.89

To further general economic prosperity, Charlemagne was at pains to re-establish the great continental trade routes that had crisis-crossed Europe in the days of the Roman Empire and which had largely retreated to Byzantine eastern Europe in the early medieval period. Accordingly he anticipated the 21st century European Union by introducing a common standard of currency throughout his empire, the silver Carolingian *denarii* and standardised weights and measures. As a result, western Europe's trading arteries began  to flow once more, culminating in an upsurge of population and prosperity in the 11th century. A large scale reclamation took place of former farming areas that had been abandoned to wilderness and the population swelled from an estimated 25 million in 800 to 100 million in 1250[9].

A symptom of this renewed prosperity was that under Charlemagne and his successors western European culture experienced its first renaissance under imperial patronage. Across Europe the emperors, their courtiers and successors endowed learning, art and architecture on a Roman scale[10]. Such patronage marks a cultural epoch; from henceforth it became the expected norm that political power should be equated with patronage and inspired others to do so too – Charlemagne's contemporary Offa's royal mortuary church of Brixworth in Northamptonshire is an 8th century example, whilst in the 11th century the French and Normans would take the Carolingian Romanesque style of architecture to its glorious extreme in the form of foundations such as Caen's *Abbaye aux Hommes* and Garonne's *Abbaye de St Pierre de Moissac*.

Despite its innumerable achievements, politically the Carolingian Empire was fundamentally a simple, loosely governed entity lacking the

---

[9] Figures from Herlihy, D. "Demography", in Ed. Strayer, Joseph R., *Dictionary of the Middle Ages* (New York, 1989).
[10] The most ambitious of Charlemagne's programmes of patronage was his 'General Exhortation' of 789, the first recorded attempt in European history to provide free schooling throughout his empire via the parish priest. The degree of literacy that this programme achieved on the part of the laity is unclear, but it was sufficiently significant in its day for Alfred the Great to draw upon it as inspiration or his own literacy scheme a century later.

means to hold itself together without a strong emperor at the helm. Less than a century after Charlemagne's coronation, the empire began to collapse following the combined challenges of the weak rule of his great grandson, the unfortunately named Charles the Fat and the pressure of Viking raids. After Charles the Fat's death in 888 AD, contemporary chronicler Regino of Prum recorded how:

'After his death, the kingdoms that had obeyed him, as though bereft of a legitimate heir, dissolved from association into separate parts; and they no longer waited for a ruler given by nature, but each chose to create for itself a king from its own innards'[11].

True political stability lay in the creation of a new entity of government – the nation state, in its European form the invention of King Alfred the Great of Wessex. More than the Carolingians, the English faced a threat to their very existence as a result of the Viking menace. By 871 six out of the seven English kingdoms had been overrun and the last, Wessex, was severely embattled. Alfred's remarkable achievement in pulling victory out of defeat is covered in Chapter 8, however it is important to consider here the European consequences of the evolution of nationalism which Alfred and his successors used to unite the English and lead them to victory over the Viking invaders and eventually to the unification of England in 935.[12]

Alfred the Great from an 18th century engraving.

Before Alfred a monarch's authority was principally derived from their bloodline or the force of their personality. Although under a powerful monarch

[11] *The Chronicle of Regino, Abbot of Prum* (died 915 AD)
[12] Adrian Hasting sets out this argument in *The Construction of Nationhood: Ethnicity, Religion and Nationalism* (Cambridge University Press, 1997).

this legitimacy could be strong, it was always potentially fragile in that it required a purely passive obedience from its subjects. Alfred's vision was of a people united by a common heritage to the land they lived upon and owing obedience to a government that ruled in their name, and thus demanded obedience not simply out of tradition, but because its people perceived it to be the rightful source of authority. Alfred's Treaty of Wedmore with the Viking King Guthrum of 878 is revolutionary in the way it defines authority – Alfred is not referred to by his traditional, territorial title of 'King of Wessex' but by the more expansive *ealles Angelcynnes* – King 'of all the English nation'. By describing himself thus, Alfred is making two huge assumptions: Firstly that the formerly disparate English people now regard themselves as one nation and that, secondly, he and his dynasty are their rightful rulers. As David Starkey writes:

'It was Alfred, who in the crucible of the Viking invasions, had forged an idea of England that was more than simply cultural and linguistic, it was political as well. Or rather, uniquely in Europe at the time, it was a combination of all three. In other words, *Aengla Land* was to be a nation state'.[13]

This concept of an English nation state would prove extraordinarily enduring, surviving successive Viking and Norman invasions within two centuries of its inception. Debatably Denmark was the next nation state, its sense of identity and political structures being unified by King Harald Bluetooth in conscious imitation of England in the late 10th century. Exactly when the people of the rest of Europe became self aware of their identity within a nation state is a matter of ongoing controversy. The most optimistic historian of the subject, Susan Reynolds, believes that France, Burgundy, Germany, the Netherlands, and Italy all develop a sense of nationhood during the medieval period[14].

---

[13] Starkey D. *The Monarchy of England* Vol. 1 (London, 2004) p. 69
[14] **Reynolds S. *Kingdoms and Communities in Western Europe, 900-1300* (Oxford University Press, 1997)**

When does the Early Medieval period end?

As with any timeframe created by historians, there is no neat end point to the early medieval period. Rather the end is the result of a series of overlapping processes which are largely completed by the end of the 10th century:

- Politically, western European kingdoms become more stable and long lasting, partly through greater sophistication of central government, partly because rising population meant greater taxation and hence more powerful government, and in some cases because of the development of an early form of nation statehood.

- Socially, the feudal system had emerged as the standard system by which society and labour were regulated; the last major kingdom to embrace feudalism was England in the aftermath of the Norman Conquest of 1066. Feudalism would remain largely unchallenged until the acute labour shortages caused by the Black Death in the 14th century.

- Economically, thanks to Charlemagne's legacy, Europe was once again part of a trade network and the early medieval regression to purely local commerce was reversed. Throughout this period, and before and after it, the majority of Europeans remained subsistence farmers, but nonetheless even in the 11th century embryonic banking systems and trade routes in commodities such as wool and spices provided glimpses into the evolution of a capitalist future.

- Culturally, after centuries of defending its very existence, western Christendom finally moves onto the offensive during the 11th century. The aggressive Normans, who conquered southern Italy and England during this period, used their brand of Romanesque architecture as a statement of cultural superiority over their subject peoples in a manner identical to the Romans – surviving buildings such as Durham and Ely cathedrals continue to loom over their landscapes today. Elsewhere European art begins to re-engage in forms forgotten since classical times such as monumental sculpture, whilst in theology strident new ideas challenge the largely evolutionary mimesis of the early medieval period. The most revolutionary of these was Pope Urban II's call for the First Crusade in 1095 in which he declared that war, hitherto automatically a sin, could actually be a sacred duty – the beginning of various theories of holy war which continue to affect humanity today.

Contemporary illustration of the First Crusade of 1095-98 which redefined relationships between Catholicism, Eastern orthodoxy and Islam.

- Finally, the sole truly European institution, the Roman Catholic Church, also asserted itself in a new, confident manner. Aggressive missionary campaigns were systematically eliminating the remnants of paganism in northern Europe, whilst in the south the *Reconquista* to liberate Spain from Islam had begun. At the centre of Church government, decades of corrupt popes and over powerful Holy Roman Emperors had reduced the papacy to little more than a figurehead in the 10th and early 11th century. The period of Hildenbrandine reform in the latter half of the 11th century would see the Church reassert its independence, purging itself of corrupt practise such as selling ecclesiastical offices (simony) and increasingly asserting itself against the ambitions of Christian kings, even the emperor himself. The landmark excommunication of Emperor Henry IV in

1076 by Pope Gregory VII, the first excommunication of a reigning European king, drew the political battle lines between the ambitions of a powerful Church on the one hand and ambitious princes on the other. This battle line would dominate the rest of the medieval period in Western Europe. The most prominent sign of this newly aggressive church was the establishment in 1099 of what was essentially a papal empire in the Middle East in the form of Crusader states which subjected much of the holy lands of Christianity, Judaism and Islam to Christian rule for the first time in nearly four centuries.

In the middle of all this change one more seismic event quietly occurred – the formal schism of the Catholic and Orthodox churches in 1054. By declaring that they were no longer part of a single Christian body, the eastern and western churches broke the last formal link that connected the Greek east and Latin west of Europe. Informal alliances and trade would, of course, continue, but this action nonetheless represents a formal and irrevocable split of two worlds which had progressively drifted apart since the fall of the western empire 500 years earlier, a split which would decisively shape how the two halves interacted with each other and the rest of the world to the present day. This then would seem as good a date as any to choose as the end of the early medieval period.

Pope Leo IX – his decision to excommunicate the leader of the Orthodox Church in 1054 led to the 'Great Schism' between eastern and western Christianity and debatably the end of the Early Medieval period.

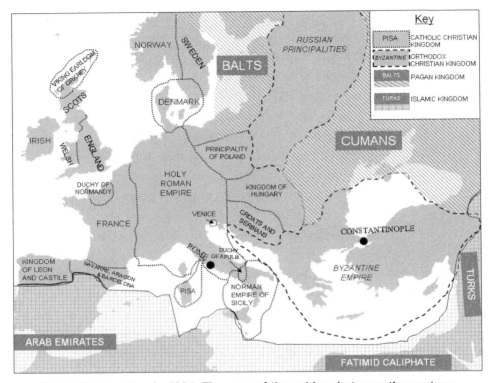

Fig.3: Christendom in 1054: The year of the schism between the eastern and western Churches

Chapter 2: The Migration Period in Britain 410-c.600

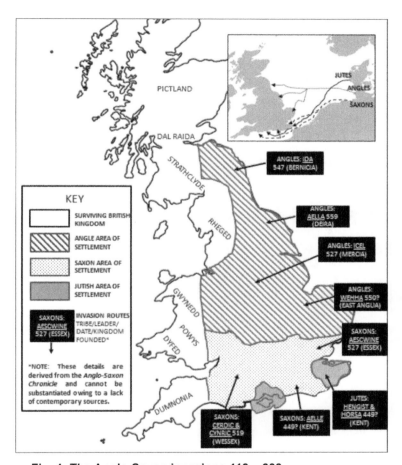

Fig. 4: The Anglo-Saxon invasions 410 – 600.

The early medieval period was dominated by the memory of the fallen grandeur of the past. For half a millennium up to the end of the 4th century AD European history was dominated by the rule of the Roman Empire. In the case of Britain, the period of Roman rule formally ended in 410AD when the Roman Emperor Honorious instructed the Britons to look to their own defences, the contemporary sack of Rome by the Visigoths requiring him to withdraw troops from the outlying regions of the empire to defend Italy.

By this point the Romanised people of Britain were already facing seaborne attack from coastal dwelling Germanic tribesmen from modern Denmark, Germany and the Netherlands – Angles, Saxons, Jutes, collectively known to history as the Anglo-Saxons. There followed a span of nearly two centuries known by historians as 'the migration period' during which these raiders became conquerors, spreading out across most of the land we know refer to as 'England' and driving the Celtic speaking Britons north and westwards into modern Cornwall, Wales, Cumbria and Scotland.

Welsh historian Geoffrey of Monmouth's 12th century legend of the white dragon, of the English, defeating of the red dragon, of the Britons, in a prefiguring of the Anglo-Saxon conquest. Even in medieval England, the events of the Migration period were clouded by myth and legend.

The invaders were illiterate pagans who brought alien, tribal notions of government and a simple, pastoral pattern of living. As a consequence the towns and infrastructure of Roman Britain fell into decay. Our historiography is almost non-existent. Anglo-Saxon historians writing centuries later provide scanty accounts of the conquerors and the semi-legendary names of their leaders – Hengist and Horsa, Angle conquerors of Kent, Cerdic and Cynric, ancestors of the Kings of Wessex etc. However even the earliest of our historians, Bede [15], was writing two hundred years after the events he portrays, using sources now lost to us. As such Bede's accounts must be treated with the same caution that a modern historian writing an account about the Napoleonic Wars on the basis of memory would merit. Our solitary

---

[15] Bede *Ecclesiastical History of the English Nation* compiled in the 730s.

contemporary source, the British polemicist monk Gildas[16] writing sometime in the period 480-550 unfortunately does not provide any detailed record, his intention being to harangue his contemporaries for the sins that apparently led God to unleash a plague of Anglo-Saxon invasion. Gildas does however provide a compelling flavour of the fear, confusion and chaos that resulted from the collapse of the urbanised, ordered Roman way of life in Britain:

'All the columns were levelled with the ground by the frequent strokes of the battering-ram, all the husbandmen routed, together with their bishops, priests, and people, whilst the sword gleamed, and the flames crackled around them on every side. Lamentable to behold, in the midst of the streets lay the tops of lofty towers, tumbled to the ground, stones of high walls, holy altars, fragments of human bodies, covered with livid clots of coagulated blood, looking as if they had been squeezed together in a press; and with no chance of being buried, save in the ruins of the houses, or in the ravening bellies of wild beasts and birds.'[17]

Beyond this, we are dependent upon physical, as opposed to written evidence, for our understanding of this period. As such it belongs to the realm of archaeology and anthropology rather than history.

Two contemporaneous processes beginning at the end of the 6th century allow us to reengage with the era as historians:

1. The gradual coalescence of tribal lands into semi-organised Anglo-Saxon kingdoms, such as Kent and East Anglia.
2. The return of Christianity in the form of a series of missions beginning with Augustine's arrival in Kent in 597. The literate missionaries and their followers spread literacy as well as faith and with it the possibility of permanent government based on the written record, beginning with King Ethelbert of Kent's laws of 602-3, the earliest written evidence in English history.

---

[16] Gildas *On the Ruin and Conquest of Britain* (c. 480-550)
[17] Ibid. Line 24

Victorian illustration of Augustine of Canterbury preaching to the people of Kent.

Despite this law code and adoption of Christianity, Ethelbert and his successors were essentially still tribal leaders rather than rulers of formal kingdoms. The process of state formation which would bring the migration period to an end began at the opposite end of the future England, in Northumbria. Before looking at Northumbria however, we need to consider the traditions of kingship and hierarchy out of which the first true English kings emerged.

Chapter 3: Kingship and hierarchy in Anglo-Saxon England

Anglo-Saxon notions of kingship

As Roman authors inform us, Pre-Conquest Germanic kingship was a markedly egalitarian concept in contrast to the rigid hierarchy of the Roman Empire and its institutions. Many 'kings' were elected by the community, and in all cases loyalty was to the individual primarily, rather than his dynasty. Male relatives of the king were not 'princes' as such, although they might be nominated as an *aethling* or potential heir of the king by his council who would decide between the claims of the *aethlings* on the death of the king. Even when Catholicism re-introduced a level of Roman style hierarchy to Anglo-Saxon society form the 7th century onwards, elements of this consensual style of kingship lingered on to the end of the period. In 1066 Earl Harold Godwinson of Wessex was named King in defiance of the claims of the only male blood relative of the previous king, Edgar the *Aethling* who would by later medieval ideas of primogeniture[18] have been the uncontested heir to the throne.

Within this system of elective monarchy a king was required to consistently prove himself worthy of the office in the eyes of his subjects, particularly his nobles whom he depended on for nearly all government and who would either ignore his authority or even assassinate him, if they deemed him unworthy. The king's fragile authority rested on two pillars – his ability in war and his generosity to his subjects in peace, in particular the men who formed his circle of warrior companions, the *gesith*. These *gesith* were at the heart of such central government as existed, deputising for the king and protecting his person – combined ministers and bodyguards. Their loyalty was legendary; the honour code of the *gesith* insisted that death was preferable to abandoning one's lord. In return they expected regular and substantial reward – their word for the king was the *sinc-gyfan* or 'ring-giver', referring to the presentation of gold and silver arm rings in return for service. The great

---

[18] The practise of the eldest son inheriting the throne followed by their son etc. and succession only passing to subsequent sons if the line of the eldest died out.

Anglo-Saxon epic *Beowulf* summarises the relationship:

So the chief that is young, by kindnesses rendered
The friends of his father, with fees in abundance
Must be able to earn that when age approacheth
Eager companions aid him requitingly,
When war assaults him serve him as liegemen:
By praise-worthy actions must honour be got
'Mong all of the races.[19]

This open-handedness neatly translated into the network of cashless patronage that defined the government of a medieval king, hence following the Norman conquest of 1066 the Anglo-Saxon system of government was retained and adapted by a successive generations of medieval kings until the professionalisation of government by Henry VIII's minister Thomas Cromwell in the 1530s.

Kingship Emerges

By the early 7th century the rank of king had clearly strengthened, as the evidence of the Sutton Hoo burial indicates. This grave in Suffolk is almost certainly that of Raedwald, ruler of the heptarchic kingdom of East Anglia and hailed by later historians as a *bretwalda* or 'overlord' of all the English kings. The immensely rich grave goods hint at a wealthy and organised society – the gemstone bedecked gold jewellery is the finest of its kind in Europe whilst the presence of coins from Merovingian France and a dish from the distant Byzantine Empire indicate established trade and diplomatic links. There is, moreover, evidence of a more formal sense of kingship in the royal regalia that was found in the tomb including a sceptre and crown. One item looks back to a more egalitarian, war-like past – a gilded helmet, symbol of an Anglo-Saxon war leader. The fact that the name of this helmet, the *cynehelm*, became the Old English word for 'crown' suggest that the memory of this early phase of kingship was never entirely forgotten.

---

[19] *Beowulf* Book I 'The life and death of Scyld' verses 20-26

The face of Anglo-Saxon kingship: the *cynehelm* from the Sutton Hoo burial discovered in 1939.

The contemporaneous introduction and ultimate domination of Roman Catholic Christianity completed by the Synod of Whitby 663 extended the concept of kingship still further. The Catholic faith had preserved the strictly hierarchical traditions of Roman government and taught that kings were chosen by God and as such were accountable to Him alone. The attraction of this untrammelled authority to the heptarchic kings is obvious, and the historian Bede provides evidence of how the Papacy and its representatives consciously courted them with the promise of divine support for their authority. In a letter of 601 he quotes a letter from Pope Gregory the Great to Aethelberht of Kent, the first king to convert to Christianity, 'Almighty God advances good men to the government of nations, that He may by their means bestow the gifts of His loving-kindness on those over whom they are placed.'[20].

With Christianity also came literacy. As a result the newly Christian heptarchic kings were able to develop rudimentary formal governments in which their instructions could be relayed to their subjects via the written word. It is also during this period that we see the emergence of the first formal rank of nobility within heptarchic kingdoms – that of *earldomen* who acted as regional governors on the king's behalf in peacetime and commanders of the army in war.

As a result of these developments, royal dynasties in control of centralised systems of government, as we would recognize them, were firmly implanted in the English kingdoms by the 7th century. Despite this, the authority of Anglo-Saxon kings was never as absolute as the Romans before them or the Normans after them. As Humble writes, in all kingdoms, some tradition of rule by consent persisted depending on 'the fulfilment of an unwritten social contract between ruler and ruled. It was not enough for a king to be a respected leader of the host in war; he also had to "be a good lord" to his subjects. This entailed constant demonstrations of justice, reliability, accessibility and speed to reward good and faithful service and punish wrongdoers'[21]. Although the principle of a single royal dynasty ruling a kingdom was rarely challenged, the nobility of that kingdom did reserve the right to depose one member of that family and replace him with another, if it deemed the former was not up to the job of kingship. The Cerdicynn dynasty of Wessex were particularly vulnerable to this – even Alfred the Great owed his throne to the intervention of the noble council or *witangameot* in the succession in 871 and he apparently narrowly survived an attempt by a faction of the same council to dethrone him in 878.

From the medieval period onwards historians have referred to this period of centralised kingdoms as the *heptarchy* - out of the multiple Celtic and English kingdoms that occupied modern England, conquest and

---

[20] Cited in Bede *Ecclesiastical History of the English People* Ch. XXXII. in E.H.D. Vol. 1.
[21] Humble R. *The Saxon Kings* (1980) pp. 19-20

intermarriage had forged seven English states by the 750s: Wessex, Mercia, Northumbria, Sussex, Kent, Essex and East Anglia. Of the Celtic kingdoms only Cornwall survived into the heptarchic period, long enough to retain its distinctive Celtic heritage, although it in turn was absorbed by Wessex in the 870s. Out of the heptarchic kingdoms, Wessex had advanced furthest down the road to statehood, certainly a factor in enabling it to survive the Viking offensives of the 9th century which destroyed the others.

Bede's *bretwaldas*

In his *Ecclesiastical History of the English People*, the historian Bede refers to a number of kings as exercising 'rule over all the southern kingdoms', a list later extended by the authors of the *Anglo-Saxon Chronicle* who also introduce the title *bretwalda* ('Britain-ruler'). The nature of the overlordship this term implies is unclear, most probably it refers to an act of nominal submission to a particular king by the other English monarchs in the form of either an oath, nominal gifts of wealth or a subservient act. In 973 King Edgar of England had himself rowed across the River Dee by the Welsh, Scottish and Strathclyder kings in such a symbolic gesture, and he may have well been drawing on a tradition from the era of *bretwaldas*:

488- c.514: Aelle of Sussex

560-593: Ceawlin of Wessex

590-616: Athelberht of Kent

600-624: Raedwald of Kent

616-633: Edwin of Northumbria

633-642: Oswald of Northumbria

655-670: Oswiu of Northumbria

829-39: Egbert of Wessex

871-899: Alfred of Wessex

The Venerable Bede from the *Nuremburg Chronicle* of 1493.

(The last two are only listed by the authors of the later *Anglo-Saxon Chronicle*)

This list is of limited utility. Not only was the title *bretwalda* never used to describe contemporary kings but it also has a clear pro-Northumbrian slant[22]; none of the three Northumbrian kings ever wielded simultaneous authority over all the rest of the heptarchy, whilst the rulers of Northumbria's great rival Mercia are omitted altogether – of these Penda, Aethelbald and Offa were at least as powerful as those on the list. Indeed Offa arguably exerted greater authority over Britain than any ruler in the pre-Alfred period. Nonetheless, the fact that Bede and the *Anglo-Saxon Chronicle*, our two main Anglo-Saxon historiographies, both felt it worthwhile to draw up a list of 'overkings' indicates that the idea of a universal ruler of all the English existed before Alfred and his descendents made it a reality in the 9th and 10th centuries.

Fig. 5: Social structures of Anglo-Saxon England

'Those who fight'

The King

Aethlings (royal heirs)

Ealdormen (senior nobles- in charge of shires)

Thegns (junior nobles – core of the army)

Hearthweru (professional soldiers)

'Those who pray'

Archbishops of Canterbury and York

Bishops

Abbots and Abbesses

Priests

Monks and Nuns

'Those who work'

Hundredmen (commoner in charge of local government)

Burgesses (merchant class governing burghs)

Ceorls (free peasants)

Slaves

---

[22] McClure J. and Collins R., Explanatory Note 77 in Ed. McClure J. and Collins R. *Bede's Ecclesiastical History* (Oxford, 2008) pp. 376-77

Chapter 4: Northumbria – the first Anglo-Saxon 'state'?

The Iding dynasty kings of the 'golden age' of Northumbria

593 – 616: Aethelfrith (Unifies Northumbria)

616-632: Edwin (puppet ruler under East Anglia)

633 – 641: Oswald (Converts Northumbria to Irish Christianity, later a saint)

641-654: Interregnum caused by Mercian occupation

654-670: Oswiu (Institutes Roman Catholic rite)

670-685: Ecgfrith (Northumbria's greatest warrior king)

685 –705: Aldfrith (literate patron of the arts)

The rise of Northumbria

The growing sophistication of royal government enabled three large kingdoms to emerge in the north, midlands and west of modern England which would dominate the heptarchy in turn: Northumbria, Mercia and Wessex. Northumbria, a huge but under-populated realm comprising most of modern northern England and some of south eastern Scotland, emerged as a power first, at the beginning of the 7th century. It had comprised three small English kingdoms, Bernicia, Deira and Lindsay and the three Celtic kingdoms of *Hen Ogledd* 'the Old North' - Catreath, Rheged and Elmet, formally locked in a permanent struggle for supremacy. The accession of the ambitious Aethelfrith of the Iding dynasty to the throne of Bernicia in 593 saw the defeat and conquest of the Celts after the Battle of Catterick in 598 and his union of the thrones of Deira and Bernicia by marrying a Deiran princess. By 615 all were subsumed into a new kingdom of *Northumbria*, literally 'north of the Humber'.

Aethelfrith's power was almost entirely military – Northumbria possessed several immensely strong fortresses such as Bamborough and Durham which served as centres of royal government. Moreover the crops of its fertile coastal strip and trade with Scandinavia funded a formidable army which established domination over both its Celtic and English neighbours in northern England as far south as the north Wales border. As a pagan king of a newly forged state, Aethelfrith's dynasty was vulnerable, depending as it did entirely upon intimidation of enemies. Thus, when he was defeated and killed by Raedwald of East Anglia in 616, his sons were obliged to flee into exile as a rival Deiran prince Edwin usurped the throne.

Bamburgh Castle, seat of the Northumbrian kings from its capture in the 6th century by the founder of their dynasty, Ida the Flame-bearer.

Aethelfrith's reign was not an innovative one – he was a pagan conqueror in the pattern of the Anglo-Saxon invaders of England over the past two centuries. Nonetheless in the establishment of the idea of Northumberland as a kingdom, he provided the context from which medieval statehood could begin to emerge in Britain and thus, 'The continuous history of Northumbria, and indeed of England, begins with the reign of Aethelfrith'.[23]

Having survived years of persecution and exile, Edwin was clearly a survivor with a ruthless instinct that rivalled Aethelfrith's. His accession to the throne of the new, semi-formed Northumbria presented huge challenges

---

[23] Stenton F.M. *Anglo-Saxon England* (Oxford University Press, 1987) p.76

however. Firstly, as a Deiran prince he struggled to establish legitimacy over the warlike Bernician nobility who were accustomed to a dominant political role. Secondly, the fact that he owed his throne to an interloper's assistance, Raedwald of East Anglia, must have further weakened his credibility.

Edwin's response appears to have been to unite the Angle nobility in a savage campaign of enforced unification against Hen Ogledd building on Athelfrith's legacy. The Celtic kingdoms of the north-west were effectively destroyed as political entities via the disbursal of their native elites and their replacement with Angle overlords. Edwin expanded further than his predecessor – as far south as the River Mersey and as far west as the Isle of Man – the first recorded case of an English king deploying a navy.

Theologically Edwin is rather enigmatic – a pagan for the first half of his reign he converted to Catholicism in 627. Bede tells us this was through the simultaneous narrow escape of Edwin from the hands of a West Saxon assassin, the birth of an heir and a divinely inspired dream. In reality, Edwin's approach to Christianity seems to have been essentially pragmatic: he was simply persuaded that it offered greater benefits in terms of divine assistance and in terms of political benefits than retaining paganism by the missionary Paulinius and by his wife, the Kentish princess Ethelburgh. In the short term his conversion brought him an alliance with Catholic Kent which enabled him to wage a successful war overthrowing his would be assassin King Cwichelm of Wessex and assert Mercian overlordship of the

A Victorian window depicting Edwain as a saintly benefactor of Christianity. In reality Edwin was just as brutal as his pagan predecessors and his conversion was most likely for cynical political reasons

south.

Longer term, the residence of Paulinus and his assistant James the Deacon in Edwin's court gave him access to literate individuals. The *Tribal Hideage*, a contemporary account of land ownership and taxation within Northumbria and beyond, has been attributed to Paulinus by N.J. Higham[24] who suggests that it is a tribute list drawn up as an aide memoire for an annual ceremony at a purpose built tribute hall at Yeavering (excavated by archaeologist Brian Hope Taylor in the 1970s and found to contained Roman theatre-style tiered seating apparently for large audiences) within which kings or their representatives from both within and beyond the borders of Northumbria would make a symbolic offering to Edwin as a token of their submission to his overlorship, an yearly affirmation of his position as universal *bretwalda* that Bede asserts:

'This king, as an earnest of his reception of the faith, and his share in the heavenly kingdom, received an increase also of his temporal realm, for he reduced under his dominion all the parts of Britain that were provinces either of the English, or of the Britons, a thing which no English king had ever done before'[25].

From his interpretation of this document Higham envisages Paulinus and James the Deacon functioning as a two man civil service, laying down the first, rudimentary layers of national government in Northumbria which would be developed in the reign of Edwin's successor Oswald. We should be wary, however, of attributing too systematic exploitation of the Catholic Church by Edwin. For all the praise lavished on him for his missionary efforts by Bede, Edwin made no effort to spread Christianity beyond the immediate confines of his court, there was no state sponsored programme of Church building and Paulinus and James were apparently the only two priests within Northumbria during his reign. Edwin seems to have viewed his conversion as a matter of short term expediency, helping him secure dominance of southern Britain and

---

[24] Higham NJ *The Kingdom of Northumbria 350-1100* (1993, Stroud)
[25] Bede *Ecclesiastical History* Book II Ch. 8 in EHD Vol. I

possibly assisting in his governance of Northumbria, but he clearly felt no great evangelising mission. Thus although Edwin was canonised by the Catholic Church following his death in battle at the hands of the pagan Penda of Mercia in 633, it seems likely that for all his notional conversion, he remained a pagan in mindset throughout his life.

Certainly on Edwin's death, Catholicism fell into abeyance in Northumbria, Paulinus fleeing into exile. Following a brief period of partition and Mercian supremacy, the first genuinely Christian king of Northumbria, Athelfrith's son Oswald would ascend the throne in 634 and it was his sincere Celtic faith, not Edwin's half-hearted Catholicism, that would spread throughout the realm.

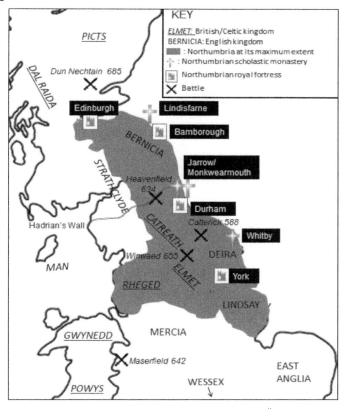

Fig. 6: The kingdom of Northumbria in the 7th century

47

Three pre-eminent Northumbrians – Oswald, Bede and Cuthbert

The legacy of medieval Northumbria was dominated by the vision of three individuals:

- King Oswald (c.604-642), who re-introduced Christianity and initiated the reforms that would evolve Northumbria as a true medieval state.
- The Venerable Bede (672-735), Northumbria's most distinguished scholar who is recognised as the father of the English tradition of history writing.
- St Cuthbert of Lindisfarne (c.634-687), a figure of such holiness that he became the *de facto* patron saint of early medieval England.

Oswald and Northumbria's rise to statehood

Despite Edwin of Deira's usurpation, the political structure of Northumbria survived and in 633 Aethlefrith's son Oswald regained the throne. As well as being a formidable warrior, Oswald was, crucially, a Christian and clearly used the conversion of his still largely pagan subjects by the Irish missionary Aidan 'the Apostle of Northumbria' to cement his own legitimacy. Medieval Christianity was doctrinally the ally of kingship - both biblical injunction and the work of early Christian theologians[26] supported the Roman idea of kingship as a natural, divinely ordained system of government. Thus culturally the newly Christianised Northumbrians were encouraged to see themselves as subjects within a permanent structure of monarchy[27]. Bede provides evidence, however, of how Oswald cannily ensured that this newfound notion of Christian obedience on the part of his diverse subjects was specifically directed at his dynasty the House of Iding, and the new state of Northumbria. Oswald achieved this by ensuring that it was *his* voice, and *his* interpretation of the Christian faith that the Northumbrian aristocracy

---

[26] St Augustine of Hippo uses the analogy of a household to explain the mutual duties of rulers and ruled: 'For they who care for the rest rule,–the husband the wife, the parents the children, the masters the servants; and they who are cared for obey,–the women their husbands, the children their parents, the servants their masters.' *The City of God* Book XIX Ch.14.

[27] "Let every soul be subject to higher powers: for there is no power but from God: and those that are, are ordained of God. Therefore he that resisteth the power, resisteth the ordinance of God. And they that resist, purchase to themselves damnation" Romans 13:1–5.

received:

'The king [Oswald] humbly and willingly... applied himself to build up and extend the kingdom of Christ in his kingdom; wherein, when the bishop, who was not perfectly skilled in the English tongue, preached the Gospel, it was a fair sight to see the king himself interpreting the word of God to his *ealdormen* and *thegns*'.[28]

We could, as Bede does, interpret Oswald's intervention as that of a truly pious king dedicated to spreading his faith. Given his astute political record however, it is more likely, however, that Oswald was aware how his authority would be reinforced by such direct association with Aidan and through him God himself. In this way he helped ensure that as paganism waned in Northumbria, taking with it residual loyalties to the monarchies of Deira, Bernicia and Lindsay. The role of Aidan's mission in the formerly Celtic provinces of Northumbria; Catreath, Rheged and Elmet; is harder to gauge as these were already Christian. The blessing of a respected Celtic scholar of Aidan's standing would certainly have helped entrench Oswald's authority over them as he inspired respect and obedience from their own priesthood. Moreover, there was undoubtedly continuity of thought and governance in these kingdoms from Roman times and as such for the Romano-Christian concept of *imperium* which Oswald was trying to instil. Finally, physical reminders of the Roman occupation abounded in early medieval Northumbria; the still useable Roman roads, Roman buildings in centres of government such as York and above all Hadrian's Wall, still a formidable military obstacle. All of these were constant reminders of a more sophisticated, organized past, a stark contrast to the subsistence and disorder of the present and an inspiration to accept Oswald's vision of a prosperous future of harmony between Celt and Englishmen, united under Christ and monarchy of Northumbria.

Oswald was not just a politician, he backed up his vision of a united

---

[28] Bede Book III Chapter III in E.H.D. Vol. 1

Northumbria with a brutally successful record as a warrior. His most spectacular victory was the Battle of Heavenfield in 634, fought in the shadow of Hadrian's Wall against a Welsh led coalition of disaffected Celtic kingdoms which resulted in the final subjugation of the northern Celtic kingdoms and their separation from their Welsh counterparts. Thus Oswald was able to fully annex Catreath, Rheged and Elmet. Whether the Celtic populations of these kingdoms were dispersed, anglicised or massacred there is no record, but from the lack of Celtic place names in northern England, their separate identity and culture were destroyed. Christian they may have been, but Oswald and his successors were certainly not tolerant. Typically, Oswald was careful that even this brutal battle should cement his reputation as a king blessed by God – the Northumbrian folk memory of the battle that Bede records devotes more time describing Oswald's piety before the battle, including erecting a wooden cross with his own hands, than it does on the event itself. Even choosing 'Heavenfield' as the name of the battle, after the site of this cross, as opposed to its geographical location near Hexham, carries obvious connotations of divinely appointed victory – there 'the heavenly trophy was to be erected, the heavenly victory begun, and heavenly miracles shown forth from this day'[29].

Heavenfield – upgraded by Oswald from a victory to a revelation of divine favour.

Oswald became the first Northumbrian 'celebrity saint' – his relics were sought after as far afield as Hildesheim Germany where this casket was created to house his skull.

---

[29] Ibid. Book III Chapter II

Beyond Northumbrian propaganda, Oswald emerges from Heavenfield with clear pre-eminence over northern England, the rulers of those places not actually subject to him acknowledged him as overlord by virtue of his Christianity. Significantly, for the first time, in Oswald we have a king of Northumbria acknowledged by Celtic as well as English sources as overlord. Indeed the contemporary Scottish scholar, Adomnán, rather grandly proclaimed him as 'ordained by God as Emperor of all Britain'.[30] Oswald also appears to have won the subjugation of the southern English kings as well, as his association with the still embryonic kingdom of Wessex indicates – not only did he marry the daughter of Cyneguils, king of Wessex, but a surviving document bearing his confirmation of the grant of Dorchester-on-Thames to the first Bishop of Wessex indicates that he wielded political overlordship.

Oswald's political and military success was short-lived. In 642 at the Battle of Maserfield on modern Shropshire, a rising Mercian monarchy under Penda, defeated the hitherto dreaded Northumbrian army. Oswald was killed and his body dismembered in an act of humiliation. Unlike his forebear Aethelfrith, however, Oswald's kingdom did not fracture of its own accord after his death in battle; evidently his programme to establish *imperium* in Northumbria had gained momentum. It survived civil war and Mercian occupation to re-emerge as the pre-eminent power in northern Britain under the rule of Oswald's brother Oswiu.

The survival of Northumbria after Oswald's death is a landmark moment in English history. For the first time a kingdom showed that it had sufficient political integrity to survive the destruction of both its ruler and its army. Northumbria had become more than simply the collective name for the possessions of the Iding monarchy, it had emerged as a self-aware state in its own right, the first in British history.

---

[30] Adomnán *Life of St Columba* Book 1 Chapter 1

Bede and the monastic scholarship of Northumbria

Although Lindisfarne was the father house of the Northumbrian monastic tradition, its greatest offspring was undoubtedly the combined monasteries of Jarrow and Monkwearmouth. Northumbrian *earldoman* Biscop Baducing seems to have conceived the foundation, according to our two contemporary sources - Bede's *History of the Abbots* and the anonymous *Life of Ceolfrid*. Using land awarded to him for military service by King Oswy at Jarrow on the banks of the river Tyne he conceived a vision of a monastery on a scale and grandeur hitherto unsurpassed in Britain. Biscop Baducing's inspirations seems to have been a series of visits to Rome and a two year stint as a monk at the Merovingian monastery of Lerins, from which he returned with a large library and a taste for the Merovingian Romanesque style of architecture which consciously copied the Roman traditions. Accordingly Jarrow, and a second monastery built at Monkwearmouth on land donated by King Ecgfrith in 674, were built in stone with glass windows using Frankish stonemasons, the use of both materials having been lost to Celts and English alike. These buildings were easily the grandest built in Britain since the fall of Rome and represented the cultural and scholastic re-engagement of Britain with mainland Europe.

A Jarrow-Monkwearmouth monk at work in the scriptorium from the *Codex Amiantinus* c.700.

Within the precincts of Jarrow and Monkwearmouth, Biscop housed his library, and we must also surmise the presence of imported continental scholars. Under their influence the monasteries effectively became early medieval universities, internationally renowned centres of learning, corresponding with, and exchanging scholars and artists with, the other great scholastic institutions of Europe, including the Episcopal school of Toledo in Visigothic Spain and the *Pandidakterion* of Constantinople in the Byzantine Empire. This cultural interchange can be seen in the glorious illuminated manuscripts originated from these institutions, most notably the Lindisfarne Gospel of circa 700 AD in which miniature portraits resembling Roman frescoes, Coptic style 'carpet pages' of cross embedded ornamentation, Greek letters and Germanic runes all feature[31]. The *Codex Amiantinus*, the earliest surviving copy of St Jerome's Vulgate Latin text of the Bible, was specifically ordered from Northumbrian scholars by Pope Gregory II in the 690s. The books of Jarrow and Monkwearmouth thus became internationally sought after works of art as well as of devotion – to the present day copies may be found across Europe. In David Starkey's words, 'The intellectual centre of the world, it seemed, had moved from the Tiber to the Tyne'[32].

Three surviving monumental crosses from medieval Northumbria at Ruthwell, Bewcastle and Easby stylistically are closely comparable to the manuscripts of Monkwearmouth and Jarrow, suggesting that the art of these monasteries was not confined solely to the written word. They feature knotwork and relief sculpture of a style also found in contemporary Irish work, suggesting that an Insular, British tradition of art ran parallel with the more cosmopolitan tradition seen in the books. Possibly this reflects the evangelising purpose of the crosses, placed in former centres of pagan worship.

Detail of the Bewcastle cross

Thus Northumbrian kings found themselves the patrons of the greatest

[31] Brown MB *Manuscripts from the Anglo-Saxon Age* (University of Toronto Press, 2007) p. 10
[32] Starkey (2004) p.30

centres of learning in northern Europe. Inevitably this must have added to the *kudos* of the Northumbrian monarchy, confirming its political and cultural pre-eminence in Britain. This can be seen in the 8th century *Gospel of St. Chad*, the greatest work from rival kingdom Mercia's first scholastic monastery, Lichfield, which is so similar in style to the Lindisfarne that until the 20th century it as was assumed to be of Northumbrian origin - imitation being the sincerest form of flattery. For the first time, an English dynasty gained an international standing too; surviving papal correspondence from the era addresses Northumbrian monarchs in a respectful style indistinguishable from that used to the great continental monarchies. Thus 8th century Pope Paul I referring respectfully to King Eadberht as 'your most prudent nobility'[33] as he would address the greatest ruling dynasties of Europe, rather than the paternalistic 'my son' reserved for lesser rulers.

The Venerable Bede (c. 673-735) was not only the greatest scholar of the dual monastery, he was the most enduring legacy of the kingdom of Northumbria. A native of Northumbria, Bede spent most of his life in the monastery. Despite his physical isolation, he was in regular communication with scholars throughout Europe and his reflections on the scriptures were internationally famed –

Bede in old age, detail from a painting by James Penrose (1902).

Pope Boniface wrote to the Abbot of Wearmouth five years after Bede's death requesting a personal copy of his works asking that the Abbot will 'Deign to have copied and sent to us certain of the works of that most skilled investigator of the Scriptures, Bede, who we have heard, hath lately shone among you... like a candle of the Church'[34].

[33] 'Letter of Pope Paul I to Eadberht, King of Northumbria, and his brother Egbert, archbishop of York' (757-8), E.H.D. Vol. 1. p. 830
[34] Letter of Boniface to Hwaetberht, Abbot of Wearmouth (746-7) Ibid. p. 825

Moreover, surviving correspondence suggests that in his old age Bede was viewed as one of the pre-eminent moral authorities in Europe. His letter to Archbishop Egbert of York, brother of King Eadbert of c. 735, is couched in the terms of a teacher addressing his pupil, not a lowly monk writing to an Archbishop. For example Bede instructs the Archbishop to 'Keep safe the flock entrusted to you from the audacious attacks of the ravening wolves, and that you remember that you have been appointed not as a hireling but as a shepherd'[35].

Bede was a prolific author, primarily theological. However it his last book for which he is primarily remembered. *The Ecclesiastical History of the English People,* completed in 731, is the first true English history, charting the history of Britain from the invasion of Julius Caesar in the first century BC to the present day. As is common amongst medieval histories, his purpose was primarily moral rather than the interpretation of the past – by tracking its process of creation and consolidation he hoped to promote the unity of the 8th century English church. But this simple objective was achieved in a work that set the standard for works of history in England for the next 700 years.

The St Petersburg script of Bede-written at Jarrow-Monkwearmouth immediately after Bede's death in 735.

The first distinctive feature of Bede's work is his methodology in the use of evidence. He describes this at the end of the *Ecclesiastical History*:

'Thus much of the *Ecclesiastical History of Britain*, and more especially of the English nation, as far as I could learn either from the writings of the ancients,

---

[35] 'Bede's Letter to Egbert c.735' in Ed. McClure J. and Collins R. (2008) p. 353

or the traditions of our forebears, or of my own knowledge, with the help of the Lord, I, Bede, the servant of Christ and priest of the monastery of the blessed Apostles, Peter and Paul, which is at Wearmouth and Jarrow, have set forth'.[36]

The writings of the ancients, the traditions of our forebears or of my own knowledge – in other words:

- existing histories, which he obtained from his monasteries' extensive libraries and through scholarly exchange with other Christian centres of learning.
- the oral history of Northumbria recorded from the now defunct bardic tradition of committing to memory and reciting, used across the world by illiterate societies to record their history and culture.
- knowledge derived from correspondence with key individuals alive in his own time.

Firstly, the skilled blending of such a diverse breadth of evidence

---

[36] Bede *Ecclesiastical History* Autobiography

The original 7th century chancel of Jarrow monastery, a remarkable survival from Bede's era where he would have worshipped with his fellow scholars.

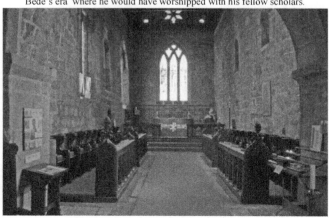

reflects a scholarly determination to record events as exactly as possible – he even records his principle sources in a preface in a manner anticipating the modern bibliography. This breadth is rendered all the more valuable as many of these sources have perished in their original form and thus survive only in his interpretation.

Secondly, the structure of Bede's history is loosely based on the example of the classical historian Eusebius. However Bede introduces several innovations which have been adopted as standard historical technique. Principally, these include:

1. The insertion of extracts from primary accounts to reinforce his analysis, including copies of papal letters obtained from the Vatican specifically for the purpose and even epitaphs on tombstones.

2. The adoption of the system of recording dates in a single chronological line from the birth of Christ which, in the form of the B.C./A.D. system we still use today. The latter replaced the previous, confusing technique of regnal dating – recording years from the coronation of the reigning monarch.

As medievalist Sir Frank Stenton recorded[37], Bede was the first Englishmen to move from the mere registration of facts to their interpretation and analysis. In other words Bede was the first English historian.

Cuthbert of Lindisfarne – the premier saint of northern England

The Anglo-Saxon Catholic church was fixated by saints and their relics. Morality and law was driven by the writings and lives of these individuals. Yet its pre-eminent native saint was, ironically, not a Catholic. Cuthbert belonged to the Celtic tradition that Northumbria maintained until the mid-7th century; a testament to the peculiar significance that was attached to his legacy.

---

[37] Stenton (1987) p.187

Unlike Oswald and Bede, Cuthbert owes his influence less to specific acts or works than to the conduct of his life. Indeed it is largely thanks to Bede's extremely detailed *Life of St Cuthbert* that built on an earlier anonymous *Life* that the latter became the centre of such an enduring cult. In life, Cuthbert was Prior of Melrose in Scotland and latterly Abbot and Bishop of Lindisfarne, the mother church of Northumbria in the latter half of the 7th century. A noted theologian, he was a disciplinarian who imposed a systematic order on the monasteries in his care. His most significant contribution to the development of the English church was an administrative one. In 663 when, following the Synod of Whitby, wherein King Oswiu decreed that the Roman as opposed to the Celtic tradition should henceforth be the religion of Northumbria, Cuthbert's acquiescence in this ensured the peaceful incorporation of all the English kingdoms into the mainstream of medieval Christian culture, thereby paving the way for the emergence of Northumbria as a pre-eminent scholastic centre of that tradition.

Latterly Cuthbert appears to have become a senior advisor to the Northumbrian monarchy, even being invited to adjudicate on who should succeed to the throne on the death of King Ecgfrith in 685. This can be inferred from his alleged prophecy of the death of Ecgfrith, made to the latter's sister Aelfrith and the advice she subsequently sought:

Episodes from Bede's *Life of St Cuthbert*. (Left) Cuthbert wades into the North Sea to coumune with sea life (Right) Cuthbert's shoes heal a paralytic.

'On hearing these words she lamented the dreadful prophecy with many tears - but then having wiped her face, she with feminine boldness adjured him by the majesty of the Holy One, that he would tell her who would be the heir to the kingdom, seeing that Egfrid had neither sons nor brothers. After a short silence, he said, " Do not say that he is without heirs, for he shall have a successor, whom you shall embrace like Egfrid himself with the affection of a sister." - "But," said she, "I beseech you to tell me where he may be found." He answered, "You behold this great and spacious sea, how it aboundeth in islands. It is easy for God out of some of these to provide a person to reign over England. " She therefore understood him to speak of Aldfrith, who was said to be the son of her father, and was then, on account of his love of literature, exiled to the Scottish islands.'[38]

Whether or not Cuthbert did indeed make a prophecy concerning the death of Ecgfrith, this account indicates that it was his influence that led to the nomination of Ecgfrith's illegitimate half-brother, Aldfrith, as his successor. Northumbrian succession had no strict rules; any man from the Iding family was theoretically eligible. That Cuthbert's nomination was not opposed by any of them indicates the tremendous level of respect accorded to him in his life.

Neither of these events form the basis of Cuthbert's extraordinary reputation for sanctity however. To Bede we owe the transmission of repeated miracles apparently wrought by Cuthbert, including Christ-like powers of turning water into wine and healing the sick. These, plus the discovery in 698 that his body remained undecomposed, fully 11 years after his death, led to his canonization as a saint. The greatest cult of sainthood in Anglo-Saxon England grew up around Cuthbert, following his body on its journey from Lindisfarne to Chester-Le-Street and finally Durham to escape Viking raids.

Bede's accounts of miracles performed by Cuthbert were embellished and supplemented by stories of those who prayed for healing at his tomb being miraculously healed. Churches as far away from Northumbria as Wells in Somerset were named in his honour, a reflection of his universal appeal for the English.

---

[38] Bede *Life of St. Cuthbert* Ch.XXIV in E.H.D. Vol. I

A modern sculpture of the flight from Lindisfarne in 793 when surviving monks carried St Cuthbert's coffin to safety. By then it was recognised as the most sacred relic in Northumbria.

The climax of the Northumbrian Monarchy

After 642 and the death of Oswald, the Northumbrian monarchy fell briefly under the domination of Penda of Mercia who controlled Deira directly and sought to ensure the loyalty of Oswald's brother, Oswiu king of Bernicia by holding one of his sons hostage.

In 654 Penda apparently decided to end the threat of the House of Iding permanently and invaded Bernicia. A combined Mercian, East Anglian and Gwynedd army duly invaded and laid siege to Oswiu in the Iding's fortress of Bamburgh. Remarkably Oswiu managed not only to resist this siege successfully but also to surprise the combined army of his enemies at the Battle of Winwaed near modern Leeds and gain a dramatic, complete victory – Penda and his ally Aethelhere of East Anglia were killed whilst Cadfael of Gwynedd fled. At one stroke, Northumbrian hegemony in the north had been dramatically restored.

Oswiu and his son Ecgfrith tried and failed to conquer northern Mercia and spread Northumbrian authority southwards but after defeat in battle in 678 the Idings concentrated on developing their control over their Northumbrian heartlands and their Celtic neighbours. Although no Northumbrian law code survives from this period, it is likely that one existed and was actively imposed as a means of projecting royal authority – Aethelberht of Kent issued one as early as 603. The *ad hoc* system of local government was partly reformed too – in the loosely confederated Northumbria established by Aethelfrith, local nobility collectively referred to as *earldomen* by Bede but in reality a diverse bunch including lesser *thegns*, semi-independent Celtic rulers and simple war lords, administered small, continually disputed patches of territory around a fortified manor complex or *vir*. These *vir* unified into larger, more controllable provinces known as *scir,* the forerunner of the shire. Although the *ealdormen* retained control of government within the *scirs* their domination was diluted by a chain of larger, royal fortresses and by grants of territory throughout Northumbria to the Church known as *bookland*. *Bookland* formed the basis of a network of monasteries providing the kings of Northumbria was a steady supply of literate scholars and administrators as well as providing 'eyes and ears' to report on the activities of the nobility.

Oswiu's chief contribution to the Northumbrian state was his decision to convert from Celtic to Catholic Christianity after the Synod of Whitby in 664. This brought mixed results from the perspective of the embryonic Northumbrian state. Politically, the Catholic Church asserted its independence from the crown under the aggressive leadership of Archbishop Wilfred of York under whose tenure it developed into virtually a state within a state, its lands exempt from taxation and its personnel from Northumbrian law. Yet it still solicited endowments, and the generosity of Oswiu and his successors Ecgfrith and Aldfrith was such that by 716 the Idings had lost the ability to reward their nobility in the traditional Anglo-Saxon manner and they were deposed by a coalition of their own followers who sporadically fought over the throne for the next 150 years.

Wilfred's crypt at Hexham modelled on Roman originals, possibly designed to house relics of St Oswald. Wilfred's enhancement of the power of the Church came at the expense of the Iding monarchy.

Culturally however, Whitby produced a remarkable effect – the Northumbrian Renaissance. Building on an already vibrant Celtic tradition, Cuthbert and Wilfred developed links across Christendom which enabled the development of a network of scholar monasteries along the north eastern coast whose outpourings represent the pinnacle of artistic and academic achievement in 8th century Europe – Jarrow-Monkwearmouth was the greatest, but Lindisfarne, Hartlepool and Whitby also made their own unique contributions.

The Lindisfarne Gospel completed c. 700, the greatest treasure of Northumbria's Renaissance.

It is also likely that is was through the continental influence of the scholar monasteries that Northumbria pioneered the introduction of a state coinage in the 750s, the first in Britain since Roman times. The new silver currency, known as the *sceatta,* was essentially a prototype penny.[39] The first were issued bearing the combined names of King Eadberht his brother

[39] Lyon CSS 'A reappraisal of the seatta and the styca coinage of Northumbria' in *The British Numismatic Journal* (1955) Vol. 28 No. 16 pp. 227-228

Echberht, Archbishop of York, the senior clergyman of Northumbria, suggesting that this coinage representing the conjoining of royal and Christian power.

Northumbrian *Sceattas*, the first Anglo-Saxon coinage produced from 680 onwards.

Centrally controlled government, a cultural and scholastic tradition of international standing, a national religion, universal law, and a common currency had thus all be achieved in Northumbria by the mid-8th century- the essential ingredients of a medieval state. It lacked as yet a sense of nationhood however – its inhabitants at best considered themselves unified by their obedience to the rule of the Idings and were prone to breaking away from Northumbria altogether to form splinter kingdoms. Moreover, by the time the introduction of common currency had been achieved, Northumbrian hegemony of the north was waning. In 685 Northumbrian ambitions of conquering the Celtic north came to a decisive end when King Ecgfrith and his army were defeated and slaughtered north of Edinburgh by the Picts at the Battle of Dun Nechtain.

Ecgfrith's successor Aldfrith presided over a golden age of Northumbrian history. Bede describes him as *sapiens* – a literate scholar. If so he was possibly the first literate king in English history. Uninterested in conquest, Aldfrith actively patronised the Northumbrian scholastic monasteries, possibly contributing writings himself. In his reign the greatest artistic achievement that survives from the kingdom of Northumbria was produced – the *Lindisfarne Gospels*. A poem attributed to him survives in a later Middle Irish form which appears to provide his constitution for wise government over a kingdom:

"Learning merits respect.
Intelligence overcomes fury.
Truth should be supported.
Falsehood should be rebuked.
Iniquity should be corrected.
A quarrel merits mediation.
Stinginess should be spurned.
Arrogance deserves oblivion.
Good should be exalted."[40]

Sadly Aldfrith's constitution for Northumbria did not long survive his death. In the fratricidal conflict for the Northumbrian crown that disfigured much of its 8th and 9th century the kingdom became at times a virtual satellite of the newly formed Carolingian Empire as its emperor Charlemagne sought to balance the rising power of Mercia. Nonetheless it retained sufficient residual strength to survive as a centre of culture and as a kingdom until 867 when the Viking invasions extinguished it permanently.

---

[40] Attrib. Aldfrith trans. Ireland, C. *Briathra Flainn Fhina Maic Ossu* (Arizona, 1999)

Historiography

Medieval:

Nennius (Bernicia only)

Bede's *Ecclesiastical History of the English People* (contemporary)

The Anglo Saxon Chronicle (two centuries later)

Current debate:

F. M. Stenton, in *Anglo-Saxon England* (Oxford University Press, 1971) p. 76 believes that the unification of Northumbria by Athelfrith represents the beginning of continuous English history in that, under him, Germanic tribal tradition begins to be replaced by national government, a process which would steadily develop under the Iding dynasty and form the basis of all later Anglo-Saxon states.

However, M. Adams *The King in the North: The life and times of Oswald of Northumbria* (London, 2013) argues that Northumbria's most significant legacy was religious and cultural rather than political – the cults of St Cuthbert and St Oswald forming a defining part of Anglo-Saxon identity; hence the profusion of churches named after them far beyond Northumbria.

N.J. Higham's *The Kingdom of Northumbria AD 350–1100* (Stroud, 1993) suggests that Northumbria survives as a coherent political and cultural identity through the conquests of Vikings and Wessex in the 9th century, as shown by the persistence of unique institutions such as the wapentake system for subdiving counties. It only looses this uniqueness with the Norman conquest.

D. Rollason's *Northumbria, 500–1100: Creation and Destruction of a Kingdom* (Cambridge University Press, 2003) disagrees with Higham, arguing that although formidable in the 7th century, ultimately Northumbria failed to develop as a state and therefore was destroyed in the later Anglo-Saxon period.

Questions to consider

- How great was the contribution of the monasteries of Monkwearmouth and Jarrow to the cultural achievements of Northumbria up to 735?

- 'The writings of Bede were the main cultural achievement in late seventh-century and early eighth-century Northumbria.' Discuss.

- How are the cultural achievements of Northumbria up to 735 best explained?

- How substantial was the supremacy of the kings of Northumbria over the rest of England in the period c. 593–c. 670?

- Why did the kingdom of Northumbria dominate seventh-century England?

Chapter 5: Mercia's imperial ambitions

Iclingas dynasty kings of the Mercian *Imperium* period

626-655: Penda – Last pagan king and first *bretwalda* of Mercia

655-58: Northumbrian control

658-675: Wulfere – patron of St Chad, second Mercian *bretwalda*

675-716: Mercian 'dark ages' – succession of short lived kings

716-757: Aethelbald – third Mercian *bretwalda*

757: Beornred – an apparent usurper defeated by Offa

757-96: Offa – fourth Mercian *bretwalda,* greatest king of Mercia, builder of Offa's Dyke.

787–96: Ecgfrith – Co-regnant with his father from 787 but died within months of him

796 –821: Coenwulf – last Mercian *bretwalda,* assumed title of 'emperor'

821-23: Ceolwulf – Coenwulf's brother of Coenwulf, dethroned and possibly murdered

823-26: Beornwulf- Usurper from a rival dynasty

Fragile foundations

King Penda of Mercia's wars against Northumbria in the first half of the 7th century form a backdrop to a process of conquest and consolidation that would see his kingdom, centred on the royal fortress of Tamworth expand to fully annex central England, establishing borders with Wessex, the Welsh kingdoms, East Anglia and its arch-enemy Northumbria. Christian sources such as the *Anglo-Saxon Chronicle* paint Penda's Mercia as a large but unstable *imperium*, incoherent in culture and bound together solely by military force and the tenuous loyalty of its nobility to the royal dynasty of the Iclingas. Whilst it lacked the binding force of a universal law code or a state sponsored Catholic Church, Mark Singer makes a compelling case for a unique experiment by Penda in *pagan* statecraft[41] – in the mixed economy of a Celtic Christian Northumbria and a Catholic Kent, he suggests that Penda consciously sought to differentiate the Mercian state he was trying to create by the imposition of a universal cult worshipping the Allfather god Woden. – an evolution of the Germanic tribal principle 'sacral kingship' in which the king was chief priest and communicator with the gods as well as political ruler.

If this is the case, even by the end of Penda's reign the isolating effects of continued paganism in the face of the remorseless encroachment of Roman Catholicism seem to have become apparent. Penda apparently raised no objection to his son and heir Wulfere's conversion to Catholicism, a tacit admission perhaps that his experiment had failed. Penda's death at the hands of the resolutely Christian Northumbrian king Oswiu at the Battle of Winwaed in 655 in any case marked the incontrovertible defeat of paganism. After this date the leaders of the Anglo-Saxons, if not the people as yet, renounced the religion of their ancestors permanently.

Anglo-Saxon belt buckle depicting Woden. Penda was his last major royal adherent.

Wulfhere succeeded to the Mercian throne in 658 following a civil war in which he overthrew Northumbrian governors appointed by Oswiu. An early step in consolidating his grip on power was the appointment of the Northumbrian trained missionary and first Mercian bishop Ceadda (later St. Chad) to lead a systematic process of conversion amongst his subjects from his base at Lichfield. Like his father, Wulfere maintained the boundaries of tribal kingdoms Mercia had subjugated as regions within the Mercian

---

[41] Singer M.A. 'Holding the Border: Power, identity and the conversion of Mercia' (MA thesis University of Missouri, 2006) pp.102-108

imperium, formerly independent kings such as that of the Hwicce on the Welsh borders being demoted to 'sub-kings', effectively governors. However there is evidence that he sought to use the Church to provide supervision of these provinces by establishing a network of minsters throughout his realms which had the triple benefits of projecting his piety, speeding the conversion of his subjects and providing literate eyes and ears who could report the activities of the sub-kings and their nobility to Wulfere's capital at Tamworth. Ironically the individual to whom these establishments are accredited to is Wilfred, Archbishop of York[42] and estranged servant of the Northumbrian monarchs who appears to have served the Iclingas during his substantial periods of exile from his archdiocese.

Partly as a result of these consolidating measures, partly because of the coincidental weakness of the royal dynasties of southern Britain, Wulfere and his successor Athelbald were both able to wage successful wars of conquest and domination which secured the subjugation of the kings of Wessex, Kent, Sussex, Essex and East Anglia as client kings – *bretwaldas* of all English kingdoms south of the Humber. Indeed Stenton argues that Aethelbald's accession marks the moment when southern England began the journey to statehood pioneered by Northumbria[43].

By the standards of the time, Aethelbald had an immensely long reign – 41 years finishing in early 757. Unfortunately Bede's pro-Northumbrian slant causes him to neglect Aethelbald and his successors. Thus our knowledge of his early reign is very limited. Between his accession in 716 and the mid-730s, however, he must have embarked on an aggressive campaign of conquest and subjugation for a whole series of charters appear which hail Aethelbald with unprecedented titles: 'King not only of the Mercians but also of the provinces which are known by the general name South Angles', 'King of the south Angles' and 'King of Britain'[44]. He had clearly become a *bretwalda* in all but name.

---

[42] Stephen of Ripon *Life of Wilfred* (c.710)
[43] Stenton (1987) p. 53
[44] Cited in Kirby D.P. *The Earliest English Kings* (London, 1991) p. 130

This overlordship of southern England can be explained partly by the strength of Aethelbald's position, but also by the temporary weakness of both Wessex and Kent: While the former was facing a successional crisis following the abdication of King Ine in 726, the latter was labouring under similar uncertain conditions following King Wihtred's death in 725, which had left no clear succession. The collapse of East Anglia into three warring sub-kingdoms, following the death of King Aelfward in 749, brought eastern England into the sphere of Aethelbald's overlordship.

Mercian gold metalwork from the Staffordshire Hoard, discovered in 2010

Aethelbald's reputation has traditionally been soured by allegations of moral corruption based on a letter sent to him by the leading missionary St Boniface and countersigned by seven other bishops in 745-6. The letter details a broad range of sins, including sex with nuns and stealing Church revenue:

'We therefore, beloved son, beseech Your Grace by Christ the son of God and by His coming and by His kingdom, that if it is true that you are continuing in this vice you will amend your life by penitence, purify yourself, and bear in mind how vile a thing it is through lust to change the image of God created in you into the image and likeness of a vicious demon. Remember that you were made king and ruler over many not by your own merits but by the abounding grace of God, and now you are making yourself by your own lust the slave of an evil spirit'[45].

However Aethelbald's dislocation from the Church was clearly not permanent. A year later, in 747, Cuthbert, the Archbishop of Canterbury, undertook the unusual step of summoning a general synod of all the senior English clergy in response to papal attacks on the corruption of his archdiocese. Significantly Aethelbald was in attendance and issued privileges to Mercian churches in his own name.

The synod of 747 appears to have marked the climax of Aethelbald's power. Athelbald never translated his unprecedented overlordship of southern England into more permanent institutions of Mercian power and by the end of his long reign he was clearly losing control in key areas. He was, for instance, never able to assert control over currency in the manner of Northumbrian *bretwaldas*; *sceattas* within his sphere of control suffered from debasement of their silver content from 730 onwards leading to galloping inflation. Possibly as Boniface's letter suggests, Aethelbald was preoccupied by his own pleasures and thus failed to take a strategic view of kingship. This would ultimately have dire personal consequences. In 757 he was murdered in a palace coup by his own *gesith*. The assassination was followed by a catastrophic civil war in Mercia over the succession, something that would have been unlikely had Aethelbald succeeded in imposing institutions of universal statehood on the model of Northumbria. Longevity and luck, with regards to the weaknesses of his neighbours, would therefore seem to be the most plausible explanation for Aethelbald's temporary *bretwalda* status in southern England.

Aethelbald thus left nothing in the way of a positive legacy for Mercia. Rather the period after his death saw Mercia lose its *bretwalda* overlordship of

---

[45] 'Boniface Writes A Letter of Admonition to King Aethelbald of Mercia' (746-7) in legacy.fordham.edu/halsall/basis/Boniface-letters.asp

the southern English kingdoms who reasserted their independence in the wake of its weakness. The victor, Offa, who seized the throne at the end of 757 thus inherited a rump kingdom centred on the midlands whose long term survival was by no means assured.

Offa's reign

Like Aethelbald, Offa reigned for a long time – 757-96. However on Offa's death there was no civil war for he had remodelled his kingdom into a coherent state whose unity and sophistication surpassed even Northumbria. On one level, Offa was a brutal *bretwalda* on the same model as his predecessors – he made peace with strong Northumbria and Wessex via intermarriage, but pursued a ruthless war of conquest against weaker Kent, Sussex, East Anglia and Essex, demoting their ruling families to the rank of sub-kings. He also beheaded Athelberht of East Anglia when he tried to rebel, the only recorded case of an Anglo-Saxon king executing another from a rival dynasty.

Offa, however, had imperial pretensions of power on a greater scale than any previous English ruler. Moreover, he promoted the most consistent image of the legitimacy of his dynasty of any Anglo-Saxon ruler until the reign of Alfred a century later. Writings, artefacts, buildings, and the mighty Offa's Dyke itself are all peppered with the language of imperialism, drawn principally from the memory of Rome but also from Germanic, Byzantine and even Moslem sources.

Offa travels in imperial splendour, an illustration by Matthew Paris, an 15th century historian.

Like Northumbria, Mercia owed much of its political and cultural cohesion to the development of the Church. Like his Northumbrian predecessors, Offa recognised the prestige of the Church could be mirrored in its sponsoring monarchy. Unlike them, however, simple patronage was insufficient for Offa, who intervened directly in the Church at several levels to promote his own political agenda. In the 780s he went as far as pressurising papal legates into elevating the senior see of Mercia, Lichfield, into a short lived Archbishopric, with jurisdiction over the entire church of central England, giving him parity with the Kentish and Northumbrian royal families who had endowed the Archbishoprics of Canterbury and York respectively.

This sense of one-upmanship spread into learning too. Offa inherited a scholastic monastery at Lichfield and added another at Peterborough by 970. The scholastic output of these monasteries is of comparable quality to the Northumbrian tradition, but there is clearly more political influence at work – the most significant surviving example, the Barberini Gospels is covered in zoomorphic letters featuring imaginary creatures, such as centaurs and manticores. Zoomorphs belong to the central European Avar tradition[46]. They been adopted by the monasteries of Offa's greatest contemporary, Holy Roman Emperor Charlemagne following his conquest and it is known that the Emperor sent a portion of the Avar's treasure to Offa as a mark of affection. The decision to copy this style in the state sponsored monastery of Peterborough suggests a very deliberate attempt to culturally link Offa with Charlemagne.

The ultimate expression of Offa's grandiose vision of himself as a Christian monarch is the greatest surviving Anglo-Saxon building in Britain – Brixworth church in Northamptonshire, as seen overleaf. Of an exceptional size for its era, this church formed part of a monastery complex and appears to have been built by Offa as a royal mausoleum for his family – a unique subterranean ring crypt seems to have been constructed for the public display of royal remains. Imperial in its size, it even features carvings such as eagles

---

[46] Brown (2007) pp.53-54

taken from Roman buildings.

Brixworth church, Northamptonshire, mausoleum of the Mercian kings.

The degree to which Offa's imperial authority over the rest of the heptarchy matched his pretensions is unclear as evidence is very limited. However, the language of surviving charters indicates the existence of sub-kings, not only in the recently subjugated kingdoms of East Anglia, Essex, Sussex and Kent, but also regions within Mercia proper who administered their 'provinces' with autonomy in the manner of imperial governors, while clearly remaining under the overall control of Offa. This relationship is evinced in the dedications of charters such as the following one made by Uhtred, 'sub-king' of the Hwicce concerning land granted to one Athelmund, son of Ingild, at Stoke Prior, Worcestershire:

'I Uhtred, by the gift of God sub-king of the Hwicce... most willingly grant to my faithful thegn namely Athelmund...
'I, Offa, by the grace of God king of the Mercians, have consented to this, my sub-king's donation'[47].

---

[47] 'Charter to Uhtred, sub-king of the Hwicce to Athelmund, son of Ingild, of land at Aston Fields, Stoke Prior, Worcester' (770) E.H.D. Vol. 1 No. 74 pp.502-3.

Offa never refers to himself as 'Emperor'; indeed he never lays claim to a greater title than 'King of the Mercians'; the title *bretwalda* seems to have been awarded after his death. However, his contemporaries and successors did grant him the unique accolade 'the glory of Britain'. The leading English scholar of the era, Alcuin of York, is particularly grandiloquent, praising Offa's sponsorship of learning in a manner indistinguishable from that used towards an emperor or a pope:

'It greatly pleases me that you are so intent on education, which is now extinguished in many places, may shine upon your kingdom. You are the glory of Britain, the trumpet of proclamation, the sword against foes, the shield against enemies'[48].

By Offa' reign, the state minting of silver coins had become standard throughout the heptarchy. However, his are exceptional in the quality of their engraving, the quantity produced and their ambition, intending to be nothing less than the first universal currency in Britain since the departure of the Romans. His success can be gauged by their prevalence throughout Britain,

 and by the substitution of the Northumbria name *sceatta* for the Mercian *penny*, a term which has persisted, of course, to the present. These first pennies show a variety of imperial themes – the standard shows Offa's profile clearly modelled on the Roman emperors, a limited run by the coiner Eoba, uniquely, displays Offa's queen Cynethryth, clearly derived from contemporary Byzantine coins of the emperor Constantine VI's mother Irene. Most remarkable is the existence of gold coinage from Offa's reign, hardly ever issued in England until the 13th century. These *mancuses* are directly copied from the *dinar* of the Abbasid empire in the Middle East, even to the extent of replicating the original inscription in pigeon-Arabic and overlaying Offa's name (upside down) over

---

[48] 'Letter of Alcuin to Offa' (787-796) Ibid. No.195 p.846

that of Allah[49]. The mere existence of such a coin hints at long distance trade with the Mediterranean, suggesting that economically at least, Offa's *imperium* was recognised far beyond the British Isles.

The unique Mercian golden *mancus*, a direct copy of the Arab *dinar*.

Amidst all this evidence we have of how Offa sought to be viewed by his subjects and successors, we have one invaluable source as to how others actually saw him – the remarkable survival of correspondence between Emperor Charlemagne to the king, the first diplomatic correspondence in history. Offa's exact contemporary, Charlemagne (748-814), was the greatest ruler of continental Europe in the early medieval period, a relentless conqueror and patron of learning who united most of western Europe for the first time since the Roman Empire. For such a man to hail the Mercian king as 'Respected and very dear brother Offa, king of the Mercians'[50] indicates that Offa was viewed with something akin to imperial status in Europe, indeed this is the only recorded occasion when Charlemagne refers to another western European king as 'brother'.

Although immeasurably Charlemagne's inferior in military power, Offa's prestige was sufficient for the Emperor to contemplate marrying his son

---

[49] Carlyton-Britton P.W.P. 'The Gold Mancus of Offa, King of Mercia' in *British Numismatic Journal* (1908) Vol. 5 No. 5. p.57

[50] Roger of Wendover 'Treaty Between Charlemagne & Offa' (790) in
http://legacy.fordham.edu/halsall/source/790charles-offa.asp

Charles to one of Offa's daughters in 789, albeit Charlemagne baulked at admitting full equality by likewise pledging one of his daughters to Offa's son, Ecgfrith. The prestige that Offa enjoyed with the Church may explain Charlemagne's exceptional courtesy to Offa – the first papal mission to England since St Augustine, the Legatine Mission of 786, is effusive in its praise for the king of Mercia. Charlemagne and Offa were thus able to present a decisively influential united front at the Council of Frankfurt in 794 which saw the western, Frankish Church reassert the supremacy over the universal church it had lost at the Byzantine dominated Second Council of Nicea in 787.

Fig. 7: Mercia and her 'empire' in the reign of Offa 757-96

Offa's Dyke

The most lasting testament to Offa's *imperium* is Offa's Dyke, a deceptively simple earthwork designed to provide a continuous defence of Mercia's border with the Welsh kingdoms. Comprising a ditch and a turf wall approximately 8 metres high when constructed, the Dyke is typical of

Remains of Offa's Dyke near Presteigne, Shropshire.

Anglo-Saxon linear defences in form, but the astuteness of its placing and its sheer length – approximately 240 kilometres consistently following high ground which commands and dominates the approach to the west. Such a structure represents a feat of military engineering comparable to the much shorter Hadrian's Wall (118 kilometres) and would not be equalled in scale until the canal building projects of the 18th century.

Apparently built in the period 784-796, during peace following protracted war with the Welsh kingdoms, the Dyke is a testimony to Offa's ability to organise and command. The existence of English place names to the west of the Dyke indicates a conscious abandonment of undefendable territory by Offa, whilst modern estimates suggest that up to 30,000 people would have been required for its construction, making it one of the largest civil engineering projects in English history. Stenton contends that such a project would have required the constant presence and supervision of the king himself.[51] Surviving charters hint at the organisation within Offa's kingdom that enabled him to commission such a project – Mercia and its subordinate

---

[51] Stenton (1987) p. 214

kingdoms are divided into irregular sized provinces – *provinciae*, loosely based on tribal boundaries whose size is indicated by the area of farmland in hides.

As with Hadrian's Wall, the purpose of Offa's Dyke is open to interpretation. Whilst it did constitute a formidable obstacle to the movement of Welsh armies, Mercia lacked the soldiers to man even a small proportion of it at any one time. It may well be as much a political as a military statement, formally delineating Mercian from Welsh land and proclaiming the might of Offa and his successors by its very existence. Its formal division of Wales from what would become England marks the permanent separation of Celtic and English land in western Britain, hitherto a porous and disputed border. The geographical and cultural border of England and Wales essentially follows the same route today.

Offa's legacy

Some historians have claimed that Offa was effectively the first King of England[52] as he exerted political dominance over the whole of the future kingdom, with the exception of Northumbria and so foreshadowed the achievements of Alfred the Great and his successors by a century. This view believes that the subsequent Viking invasion delayed the process of English nation building started by Offa and required Alfred to restart rather than initiate it. Broad historical consensus rejects this view, however, arguing that the nature of Offa's realm was that of an empire, not an embryonic nation state. It was born in part by good fortune – Offa's reign coincided with a period of unusual weakness on the part of the other royal dynasties of the heptarchy which he ruthlessly exploited. As Richard Humble writes 'the essential point about Offa's supremacy as "King of the English" is that it was a one man *tour de force*, a shrewd but temporary exploitation of the weaknesses of Mercia's rivals'[53].

---

[52] Susan Abernethy's thefreelancehistorywriter.com is a modern example.
[53] Humble, R. *The Saxon Kings* (London, 1980) p. 34

Moreover, there is little evidence of any attempt by Offa to impose unity over the kingdoms he subjugated beyond the installation of complaint 'sub-kings' or ealdormen to administer them in his name. After Offa's death in 796 his successor Coenwulf, a capable if not outstanding ruler, immediately faced rebellion in Kent, resolved only by establishing his own brother Cuthred as a semi-autonomous ruler there in 799. More importantly, by 802 Egbert Cerdicynn had seized the throne of Wessex and immediately pursued an aggressively anti-Mercian policy from his kingdom which, in population, resources and strategic position was potentially a much stronger state than Mercia.

The early 9th century saw Egbert's relative military strength rise in relation to Mercia, particularly following a crisis of kingship in Mercia following the death of Coenwulf in 796 and the rapid dethronement of his successor and brother Ceolwulf by one Beornwulf. Beornwulf was not part of the Iclingas dynasty and lacked the authority to bind his disparate realm together. By 825 the East Anglians were already in open revolt, and at the decisive Battle of Ellendun, Egbert defeated the main Mercian army. Kent, East Anglia, Sussex, Essex and Essex's former province of Surrey all turned to Egbert as their protector and *bretwalda*. Mercian power was reduced to the customary borders of the kingdom, whilst Wessex assumed dominance over all southern and eastern England, a position which remained until the Viking invasions of the mid-9th century.

Historiography

Medieval:

The Anglo Saxon Chronicle

The letters of Alcuin

Nennius' History of Britain (tangentially)

Current debate:

Michelle P. Brown and Carol A. Farr, in the introduction to *Mercia: An Anglo-Saxon Kingdom in Europe* (Leicester University Press, 2001) p.5, argue for a unique culture emerging in Mercia independent of the Carolingians and thus creating one of the underpinnings of a nation state. But the Iclingas fail to develop a coherent political ideology to take their rule beyond that of simple loyalty to a dynasty. Brown & Farr also challenge Stenton's argument for the total subordination of neighbouring kings to the will of the Iclingas dynasty, believing that he mistranslates the term *regulus* as 'sub king' when 'client king' might be a better statement – implying a temporary, not a permanent acceptance of inferiority.

Michael Wood's *In search of the Dark Ages* (BBC Books, London, 2003) considers that Offa's reign represents the culmination of a process whereby *bretwalda* kings sought to consciously imitate the behaviour and lifestyle of Roman Emperors as a means of power projection – hence Roman style coinage, Hadrian's wall-esque Offa's Dyke and Romanesque Brixworth church. Offa wanted to be seen in the guise of a classical emperor rather than ruler of a united England. Wood believes this imperial theme might have developed into a Mercian led English nation state had the Iclingas dynasty not fragmented after Coenwulf's death.

Sir Frank Stenton in *Anglo-Saxon England* (Oxford University Press, 1971) agrees with Wood's assertion that Mercia's 'empire' marks the first stage in the process towards the unification of an English 'nation state'. He goes further too, arguing that the Iclingas laid down the administrative structure for such a transformation – converting conquered local kings into regional governors and that the Mercian synod of the king and all his bishops represents the first step in the creation of a national governing council or *witan*.

Questions to consider
- Who contributed more to the development of Mercia as a major power in the eighth century: Aethelbald or Offa?

- How is the predominance of Mercia in eighth-century England best explained?

- To what extent can Offa be considered King of England?

- To what extent did Offa and his successors draw upon the example of Rome in their style of kingship?

Chapter 6: The Vikings in England: The Fury of the Northmen

Key events

789: Viking raids on the English coast begin

865: Ragnarsson brothers' invasion of eastern England begins

869: East Anglia is conquered by Ivar the Boneless

871: 'Year of Battles' – unsuccessful Viking invasion of Wessex

874: Mercian king Burghred flees into exile, arrival of Viking king Guthrum in East Anglia

876: Annexation of Northumbria completed – it becomes the Viking kingdom of York

877: Eastern Mercia becomes the Danelaw

878: Defeat of Guthrum's invasion of Wessex by Alfred the Great, end of Viking expansion

902: Edward the Elder begins the reconquest of the Danelaw

954: Defeat of Northumbrian Viking king Eric Bloodaxe

924: Death of Eric Bloodaxe ends the first Viking Age in England

980: Vikings under Sven Forkbeard renew raids on England

1003: St Bride's Day massacre changes Forkbeard's policy to outright conquest

1013: Forkbeard proclaimed first Viking king of England

Origins of the *vikingr*

According to the *Anglo-Saxon Chronicle*, the sudden appearance of Viking raiders looting the Northumbrian monastery of Lindisfarne was totally unexpected and flabbergasted the contemporary English, prompting the widespread belief that they were a judgement from God. However, there is evidence of earlier, probing raids in Portland in 789 and Kent in 792, as well as extensive contact between the English kingdoms and those of the home of the Vikings, Scandinavia, in the century before this, suggesting that the Viking age was a product of evolution rather than sudden aggression.

Although our historical record is limited, from archaeology and folk memory it seems that the reason for the appearance of Viking raiders across northern Europe in the late 8th century was a combination of technology, demographics and political change. The perfection of the longship during this period gave the Scandinavians a fast, manoeuvrable vessel with a shallow draft, capable of simultaneously sailing across oceans and up rivers. Unlike other contemporary vessels, it did not require harbours and could be simply beached. It was a perfect ship for trading across the seas and rivers of northern Europe, but was even more effective as a 'hit and run' raider able to transport a small, heavily armed crew who could land, pillage the surrounding area and escape out to sea before the slow moving and largely land based armed forces of early medieval Europe could retaliate. Established trade links meant that Scandinavians would have been familiar with the coastlines of northern Europe prior to the Viking age and thus were well briefed on the most lucrative areas to attack.

A reconstructed longship, the *Hugin* in Ramsgate, Kent

Scandinavia appears to have undergone rapid population growth during the 8th and 9th centuries. Its mountainous terrain has a finite amount of agricultural land available and this prompted younger generations to journey overseas seeking new territory. The first wave of these emigrants came from Norway and it is to them we owe the collective term 'Viking' from *vikingr* – one who sails in an armed expedition. These early Vikings were few in number and typically sought out under-populated lands on the edge of Europe to settle – Iceland, the Isle of Man, the Irish coasts and the western isles of Scotland.

Viking elite warriors or *bezerkers*. The figure on the right is wearing a bearskin as armour.

Such small scale expeditions lacked the resources to challenge the comparatively populous and centralised English kingdoms. It would require a political revolution in Denmark prompted by the Carolingians to create Viking expeditionary forces of the necessary scale. Charlemagne's aggressive Christianisation of the Danes' southern neighbours, the Saxons, in the 770s eliminated the buffer zone between the resolutely pagan Danes and Christendom. Their response appears to have been to resort to increasingly centralised rule under a royal family, the House of Sigfred, who refortified the Iron Age *Danevirke*, an earthen boundary wall in the fashion of Offa's Dyke dividing Denmark from Germany. Our written sources are scarce and largely legendary, but it appears that post 770s Denmark underwent three simultaneous processes which created perfect breeding conditions for the impulse to go *vikingr*:

- Most obviously, the reconstruction of the *Danevirke* geographically and culturally isolated the Danes from mainland Europe meaning that future expansion of their growing populations would have to be seawards.

- The house of Sigfred did not achieve unified rule over the Danes until the 830s, meaning that different scions of the ruling house controlled Denmark in a shifting pattern of coalition and civil war which created a large pool of experienced warriors and the noble leadership necessary for large scale expeditions.

- As Foote and Wilson have observed[54], the structure of Danish society itself facilitated the Viking movement, being divided into administrative provinces known as *herreds* obliged to provide around forty fighting men each – the size of a typical longboat crew. There was, moreover, a tradition of consensual rule based around the institution of the open air assembly or *thing*. The core of Danish society was the freeman, a hybrid farmer-fisherman conscious of his obedience to his lord or *jarl*, but expecting protection from violence and privation in return. In the face of land shortage and population growth such mutuality provided further impulse to expand overseas.

Overall then, lacking the centralising influence of the Roman Catholic church, pagan Danish society seems to have adopted a lose federal structure of government, organised enough to sustain large scale *vikingr* expeditions, but lacking the central governance that might have restrained the raiding impulses of individual Danish *jarls* and their followers. The aggressive actions of the Carolingians towards their Saxon neighbours also hardened Danish attitudes against Christianity, creating a feeling of cultural apartness that perhaps explains the particular savagery the early Vikings showed towards

---

[54] Foote P. and Wilson D. *The Viking Achievement* (1974, London) pp. 10 -11

the clergy. For all these reasons when the English began to feel the force of Viking raids from the 780s onwards, it was a predominantly Danish foe they faced, so much so that Scandinavians tend to be grouped together in English sources under the name 'Danes'.

From raiding to conquest

From the 790s until the 860s Danish Viking raids were a steadily escalating nuisance rather than an existential risk to the English kingdoms. From 865 onwards there is an abrupt change in Viking tactics, raiding escalating towards actual invasion. The cause of this shift is unclear. The closest thing we have to a contemporary account being Saxo Grammaticus' 13th century Danish history in which he attempted to piece together disparate folk memories from the 9th century. Saxo's account states that it was the capture and brutal execution of a Danish prince, Ragnar Lothbrok, by King Aelle of Northumbria that prompted this invasion:

'His guilty limbs were given to serpents to devour, and adders found ghastly substance in the fibres of his entrails. His liver was eaten away and a snake, like a deadly executioner, beset his very heart'[55].

From the depths of his agony, Ragnar predicts that his sons will avenge him. Accordingly the Ragnarsson brothers - Ivar the Boneless, Björn Ironside, Halfdan Ragnarsson, Sigurd Snake-in-the-Eye, and Ubba rallied sufficient support from across Denmark to equip a sizeable army and fleet and use this to conquer Northumbria. Despite their improbable sounding names, the sons of Ragnar certainly existed; English accounts corroborate Danish sources at this point. But the death of Ragnar remains unsubstantiated legend. Given the loose federal structure of Denmark, it is in any case unlikely that the death of one *jarl* would have been sufficient pretext to rally the Great Heathen Army which invaded Northumbria in 865. More plausible is that protracted civil war in Northumbria had led to a power vacuum into which the

---

[55] Saxo Grammaticus *Gesta Danorum* Book 9

Vikings, under the inspired leadership of Ivar the Boneless, were able to exploit. Whatever the cause, Northumbria was swiftly annexed and in 876 the *Anglo-Saxon Chronicle* records that Halfdan Ragnarsson, the new Danish king of York, shared out Northumbrian lands to his warriors who settled and reverted to farmers.

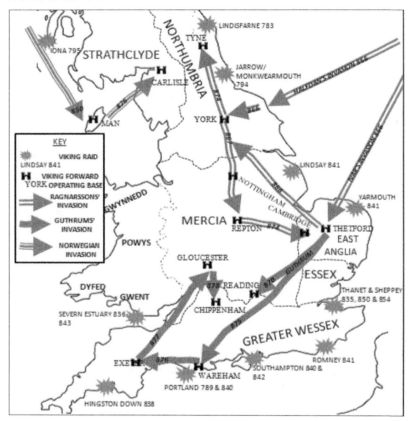

Fig. 8: The 9th century Viking invasion of Britain

How complete was this invasion? There is no doubt that the Vikings intended to rule absolutely over the land they had conquered – Aelle and several of his senior nobles were subjected to the dreadful ritual of the 'blood eagle'[56] to quell resistance. However it seems unlikely that a universal

---

[56] The victim's ribs would be hacked from their spine and their lungs splayed out behind them like the wings of a bird.

redistribution of land from conquered to conqueror took place on the model of the Norman Conquest – there were simply too few Danes. Our sole source of evidence is inconclusive - modern place names derived from Scandinavian typically ending in –by or –thwaite i.e 'Whitby' or 'Bassenthwaite' and which point to heavy concentrations of Danish settlers in all the coastal regions of Northumbria. However even in modern Yorkshire, where the largest concentration of Danish place names have been found, they account for at most 48% of the total.[57]

The Ragnarssons' invasion therefore seems to have had less of the character of a mass migration, more of the substitution of the top strata of Northumbrian society by a small but dominant class of Viking overlords. Halfdan and his successors founded a Danish monarchy which ruled from York (derived from the Danish Yorvik) between 876 and 944 which oversaw a near universal takeover of Northumbrian government by the invaders – only the great fortress of Bamburgh and its hinterland under the dynasty of Eardwulf appears to have remained under English control. Evidence for this period of Viking overlordship can be seen in the way the still loosely formed institutions of Northumbrian government took on a permanently Danish flavour – the smallest division of local government being the wapentake, an evolution of the herred, markedly bigger, from the English hundred system used elsewhere. Northern England was still divided into wapentakes two centuries later as the Domesday Book informs us.

What did this process mean for the people of Northumbria? For the great majority, other than now paying taxes to Danish jarls, as opposed to English earldomen, the change was probably not that profound. Indeed colonisation may well have been preferable to ongoing raids and enslavement. For the elite, although the most senior rank was eliminated, many of the junior, thegn class undoubtedly survived under the lordship of new masters.

---

[57] Richard J. *Viking Age England* (1991, Bath) p.33

The Church too survived in a reduced form. There is certainly no evidence of a systematic campaign against Christianity on the part of the Vikings: Though the Archbishop of York Wulfere fled the Ragnarsson's invasion in 867 he returned the next year and was allowed to govern the ecclesiastical hierarchy of the north freely. However, the Church suffered severe economic losses in terms of confiscated land and loss of patronage from disposed Northumbrian nobles.

Most grievous, however, was the cultural devastation wrought by Viking raids on the greater scholastic monasteries of Lindisfarne, Jarrow and Monkwearmouth, an unintended by-product of looting rather than a deliberate targeting of English learning. The result was nonetheless a collapse in the structure of English education – with the elimination of its Northumbrian core standards of literacy and artistic endeavour across the English speaking kingdoms plummeted. Alfred the Great, growing up in the midst of this turbulence, graphically describes its consequence: 'Learning had declined so thoroughly in England that there were very few men on this side of the Humber who could understand their divine services in English, or even translate a single letter from Latin into English: and I suppose there were not many beyond the Humber either'[58]. Even Alfred, however, concedes that this was not solely the work of the Vikings, and that a decline in learning had already set in the century prior to the invasion: 'We were Christians in name alone, and very few of us possessed Christian virtues'[59]. This view is shared by Richards who notes that one of the four great scholastic monasteries of Northumbria, Hartlepool, had been abandoned years before the Viking raids even reached it.[60]

Nonetheless, acting disproportionately as it did upon centres of learning, there is no doubt the Viking impact on English culture and education in Northumbria was devastating and irreparable. Even when there was an educational renaissance under Alfred and his successors from 878 onwards,

---

[58] Alfred *Preface to Translation of Gregory the Great's Pastoral Care* (London, 2004) p.125
[59] Ibid.
[60] Richards (1991) p. 99

it was a West Saxon, not a Northumbrian revival. Moreover it was dependent on Mercian and continental scholars for its inception, the great Northumbrian tradition of the 7th century having by this point receded into memory. The one positive consequence was that the Alfredian Renaissance was able to introduce a new and vibrant spirit of learning uninhibited by the lost culture of its predecessors – the revolutionary use of vernacular English as opposed to Latin as the language of education would have surely been far harder, if not impossible, had the legacy of the Northumbrian monasteries remained.

Southward expansion

As early as 866 the Vikings had set up forward operating bases south of Northumbria, in the kingdom of East Anglia, where a timid King Edmund was apparently induced to allow them to use his lands as a base for raiding into north eastern Mercia in return for ceasing to raid and plunder. Edmund thus became the first of many English 'puppet rulers' whose notional authority would be retained by the Vikings to lend a veneer of legitimacy to what was essentially outright conquest. Edmund's continued existence was only tolerated briefly by the Ragnarssons. Long enough, however, for them to mount a simultaneous assault on northern Mercia from southern Northumbria and northern East Anglia, creating a land bridge between their forces defended by fortified towns that would later be known as the 'five boroughs' – Lincoln, Derby, Nottingham, Leicester and Stanford.

A later medieval illumination of St Edmund being led to his martyrdom at the hands of Ubba Ragnarson.

Their supply lines thus secured, in 869 Ivar and Ubba Ragnarsson began the outright conquest of East Anglia, beginning, according to 10th century hagiographer Abbo of Fleury, with the dramatic execution of Edmund,

91

using him as a human archery target – a martyrdom that later resulted in his canonisation[61]. This brutal execution *pour encourager des autres* worked; within the year East Anglia had submitted. New puppet rulers were instituted, Oswald and Aethelred. But, as with Northumbria, a mass redistribution of land to the Viking conquerors took place. The only difference was that at some point in 875 the Ragnarssons departed back to Northumbria, leaving the rule of East Anglia to a Danish prince known as Guthrum under whose command a second wave of Viking invaders had begun to arrive.

The shield wall, standard battle formation of both Vikings and Anglo-Saxons.

Guthrum's new army was just as land hungry as its predecessors. Accordingly, in 871, a huge offensive was launched, aimed at Wessex. Fought to a standstill by the unexpectedly tough opposition encountered there, Guthrum's men switched their attention back to Mercia. King Burghred of Mercia, hard pressed by a simultaneous threat to his western border by the Welsh princes was induced to part with a massive amount of *danegeld* between 872 and 876. This crafty policy of economic warfare not only enriched the Vikings, it also impoverished Burghred, to the extent that his troops went unpaid and his authority withered. Thus in 877 what had been the largest English kingdom collapsed without a fight – its northern half, including its capital Tamworth and religious centre Lichfield, were occupied and assimilated under Viking rule. Perhaps fearful of the fates of Edmund and Aelle, Burghred fled to Rome seeking sanctuary with the papacy. Despite this,

---

[61] Abbo of Fleury *Passio Sancti Eadmundi* written under the patronage of Dunstan of Glastonbury 986.

resistance to the Vikings continued in the southern half of Mercia under the leadership of *Ealdorman* Aethelred. It is therefore more appropriate to speak of the partition of Mercia diagonally along its north west – south east axis. The southern half remained English under what effectively amounted to the kingship of Aethelred, whilst the northern half was placed under the notional authority another puppet, 'a foolish kings' thegn'[62] called Ceolwulf who took his orders from Guthrum.

By the end of 877 therefore, the only intact English kingdom still defying the Vikings was Wessex, under its king, Alfred. The attempts by Guthrum and his successors to annex this last, most lucrative kingdom will be considered in more detail in the following chapter on Alfred. Before considering this it is necessary to discuss the nature of Viking rule in more detail.

Conquest or assimilation?

The Viking invasion was first and foremost a military affair. The leaders of the victorious armies established monarchies for themselves at York and Thetford (Halfdan Ragnarsson and Guthrum respectively) under whose loose federal authority semi-independent Viking warlords established themselves as *jarls* controlling tracts of land centred on fortress towns, or 'burghs', within four 'states' collectively known as the Danelaw – the kingdoms of York and East Anglia, the Five Boroughs and Danish Mercia. That these *jarldoms* successfully dominated the area and were able to levy frequent tax off the population can be inferred from the repeated raising of substantial armies within the Danelaw over the next fifty years. Who was actually paying this tax is harder to identify given no tax records from the Danelaw have survived. As previously mentioned, evidence for the density of Danish settlement is primarily based on the uncertain record of place names. To this we can add the proportion of Scandinavian personal names in official documents and the number of Viking burial sites. From these imperfect sources, south of

---

[62] *Anglo-Saxon Chronicle* entry for the year 877 E.H.D. Vol. 1

Northumbria, we have evidence of substantial Norwegian migration on the Wirral peninsula near Chester on the west coast of Mercia, and substantial Danish settlement on the coast and hinterland of Suffolk in East Anglia and the modern counties of Derbyshire, Nottinghamshire, Leicestershire and Lincolnshire in Mercia. This is enough evidence to suggest that after the armed invasion came a wave of Scandinavian economic migrants in search of farmland, but nowhere near enough to swamp the English population, even in the areas of heaviest settlement.

Fig. 9: The Danelaw at its maximum extent circa 900 AD.

Richards' view[63] is of a landscape under firm Viking overlordship, but with actual control of the land largely remaining in the hands of the English *thegn* class and peasantry inhabiting scattered settlements, interspersed by more nucleated, turf walled and defendable Scandinavian settlements, such

---

[63] Richards (1991) pp.30- 42

as Goltho in Lincolnshire. The overall effect would have been similar to the frontier towns of mid-west America in the 19th century.

Given the small size of the English population in the 9th and 10th centuries, there was certainly enough land to go around. Thus this limited encroachment does not seem to have led to serious economic hardship for English farmers within the Danelaw. On the contrary, in fact, in the short term their lives may have become economically a great deal easier – the last generation of English rulers, pressed as they were for extortionate *danegeld*, must have been harsh taxers of their people and, of course, the pillage and enslavement to which rural English population had been subject to for three generations by Viking invaders also ceased. Up to the 910s, when Alfred's children, Edward and Aethelflead, began to make serious inroads into the Danelaw, the burden of Danish government on the English was relatively light. Thereafter the need to raise constant armies caused a dramatic increase in taxation for English and Viking farmers alike. This may explain the surprisingly positive reception given to the Cerdicynns' conquest of East Anglia and Mercia by its Danish settlers in the early 10th century – by this time many of them were Christian and clearly felt more affinity towards an English government with a mandate for peace and unity than a divided Viking leadership which offered only extortion and ongoing war[64].

The effect on the small English urban population is more mixed. Anglo-Saxon towns had undoubtedly suffered as a result of Viking raids, twice over in fact, for such raids dislocated the trade routes with the continent that formed the basis of their wealth. On top of this they bore a disproportionate burden of the taxation levied to try and fend off this threat too. As a result some such as the recently built port of Southampton withered away almost to nothing, whilst others, notably London, which occupied strategically important sites, decayed as trading towns and instead reverted to the position of Viking strongholds. Towns of economic benefit to the Vikings however, thrived such as Thetford, Cambridge and Norwich. Above all, the principle city of the Danelaw, York

---

[64] *Anglo-Saxon Chronicle*, entries for the years 919-920 E.H.D. Vol. 1

experienced an unprecedented boom, its population more than doubling to an estimated 10,000[65]. Loyn attributes this not only to the peace and cessation from raiding that Viking conquest brought, but also the new markets opened up by Viking seafaring skills, from Iceland and Greenland in the west, to the rivers of modern Russia in the east[66]. It is therefore in terms of a realignment of trade routes from the south east to the north east rather than their destruction that we should view the long term consequence of the Viking invasions of the 9th century. Although Scandinavian settlers undoubtedly befitted from these new trade arteries, so too did the English – modern excavations of Viking era burials under York Minster have found no evidence of a racially segregated population, indeed the burial rites of rich Vikings and English appear so similar as to be virtually indistinguishable from each other[67].

Reconstruction of the Viking trading hub of Jorvik.

Aside from the initial period of conquest and terror, the economic

[65] Figure from Loyn H.R. *The Vikings in Britain* (Tiptree, 1977) p. 134
[66] Ibid.
[67] Richards (1991) pp.110-111

impact on the English population of northern and eastern England of the Viking invasions appears to have been limited. In the case of English and Viking settler alike, loyalty to a particular ruler seems to have been based less on ethnicity, more on that ruler's ability to bring peace and their willingness to meet the needs of the local population. Thus, as we have already observed, Mercian Danes in the 910s and 920s happily submitted to the rule of the Cerdicynns, but in the unique case of Northumbria the reverse was true, with the local English population having more affinity and loyalty to the Danish king Eric Bloodaxe in the 940s and 50s than to the imposition of southern English rule in the form of Edmund of Wessex.

The peaceful assimilation of Viking settlers into mainstream English society was recognised by Alfred and his successors when they reconquered the Danelaw. Neither massacre nor deportation accompanied this process. The habit suggested by a later law code of Edgar[68] from the 960s was that they should be governed by their own laws and be responsible for their own conduct under the supervision of a *Jarl* of the Danelaw who was responsible to the king in the manner of any other English nobleman. This accommodation was assisted by the progressive conversion of the settlers from paganism to Christianity in the early 10th century, in part impelled by the example of their leaders, in part by the need to convert in order to take English wives, and partly to further their business interest with Christian trading partners[69]. In addition to religious practises, conversion also brought Viking settlers within the tradition of patronage and endowment of the Christian institutions they formerly looted, a central component in medieval English culture. Indeed, from the mid-10th to the mid–11th century, Scandinavian immigrants not only endowed churches and monasteries but brought their own innovations, such as 'stave churches' constructed of split oak logs originating in Norway (an example survives at Greensted in Essex.[70]

---

[68] Article 2 of Edgar's law code issued at "Wihtbordesstan" (IV Edgar 962-3) E.H.D. Vol. I p.435
[69] Richards (1991) p. 118
[70] Foote P.G. and Wilson D.M. *The Viking Achievement* (London, 1974) p. 420

Scandinavian style 'stave building' in Greensted Church, Essex. Built in the late Anglo-Saxon period between 845-1055, it is the oldest surviving wooden church in the world.

Christianity brought these Viking settlers within the mainstream culture of England and Europe in general, thereby establishing further division between themselves and Scandinavians who retained the raiding, pagan *vikingr* lifestyle. Only from 1000 onwards would the brutal, spectacularly ill-advised policy of stirring racial hatred by Aethelred the Unready unravel a century's legacy of co-existence between Viking and Englishman.

The Bloodaxe rebellion

Athelstan's victory at the battle of Brunaburgh in 937 marked the formal end of the process of English unification. Within years, however, the dispossessed Viking kings of York were actively fermenting rebellion from the Irish Viking colony of Dublin, with a view to regaining their kingdom.

In the midst of this relative harmony there is one jarring note – the Northumbrian Eric Bloodaxe rebellion of the 940s and 50s. Closer examination shows, however, that this was not a 9th century style pagan Viking invasion; rather it was the product of the unique circumstances of Northumbria. Prior to Viking invasion, loose structured Northumbria had never been a truly coherent state, being divided along ethnic lines between English and Celts within and Scots and Strathclyders without. Nonetheless the memory of Northumbria's 7th century glory days and the prosperity of the Viking kingdom of York had bred an aggressive sense of identity on the part of a portion of the Northumbrian elite who felt more affinity for the exiled kings of York than they did the rule of the southern Cerdicynn dynasty. Accordingly, rebels comprised a curious alliance of pagan Viking adventurers led by the charismatic Bloodaxe and Northumbrian separatists led by Archbishop Wulfstan of York.

For a brief period in the 940s this unlikely coalition seized the throne of York and even threatened the Five Boroughs. Significantly however the settled Danes of the Boroughs did not rise in support, indeed the *Anglo-Saxon Chronicle* claims that 'The Danes had been forcibly subdued in bondage to the heathens'[71]. Moreover Bloodaxe turned out to be an inept ruler and the re-established Viking kingdom to York rapidly degenerated into farce as rival claimant Olaf Siggtrysson and Bloodaxe staged repeated coup and counter coup against each other, effectively turning a separatist movement into a civil war, as Jones eloquently describes: 'Like puppets on a string the Dublin contenders [Siggtrysson and Bloodaxe] came jerking across the Irish Sea. They seem hardly to have had time to strike the coins which are so eloquent a testimony to their royal pretensions, before they were on their way again'[72].

As the impetus of the conquest spent itself in futile civil war, the bulk of the Northumbrian Vikings, like their contemporaries further south, decided that their future lay in the comparative peace and strong government of the Cerdicynns. In 954 Bloodaxe died, either assassinated or, according to 13th century historian Roger of Wendover, ambushed by an Anglo-Danish alliance of *Jarl* Maccus and Ealdorman Oswulf:

Coin of Eric Bloodaxe, last Viking king of Northumbria.

'King Eric was treacherously killed by Earl Maccus in a certain lonely place which is called Stainmore, with his son Haeric and his brother Ragnald, betrayed by Earl Oswulf; and then afterwards King Eadred ruled in these

[71] *Anglo-Saxon Chronicle* entry for the year 942 E.H.D. Vol. 1
[72] Jones G. *A History of the Vikings* (London, 1975) p. 240

districts.'[73]

True or not, the sentiments of this story reflect the fact that by the 920s pagan Viking adventurers of the mould of Bloodaxe were an embarrassing anachronism, as much of a threat to the Scandinavian as the English inhabitants of the Cerdicynns' realm. With the exception of firebrands like Wulfstan, by the 920s even in Northumbria loyalty to a united English nation state was increasingly becoming the norm on the part of Vikings and English alike as Loyn writes: 'The hard work inside the southern English kingdoms, the provision of better peace, the identification of Christianised Danish farmers with the surviving Christian dynasty helped to ensure that the future hope of a peaceful kingdom rested on the House of Wessex'[74].

The Vikings return

After nearly a century of peace, Viking raids on England began again in 980. This was the result of a combination of factors – the rebuff of Viking expeditions in France, Russia and the Black Sea swung the momentum of Viking expansion westwards once more.

A romanticised 19th century view of the rebuff of the Viking siege of Paris in 886 by Count Odo. This event turned Viking eyes westward back to England.

---

[73] Roger of Wendover, *Flores Historiarum*, ed. H. O. Coxe, *Rogeri de Wendoveri chronica, sive, Flores historiarum*. Vol 1. (London, 1841) pp. 402–3.
[74] Loyn (1977) p. 67

Moreover the emergence of Denmark as Europe's second nation state under the English derived blueprint of King Sven Forkbeard added a new dimension to Scandinavian capabilities. The annexing of much of Norway to Sven's realm in 999 expanded his resources still further. No longer did private armies of Vikings raid in loose coordination; the force that ravaged England from 980 onwards was a disciplined national army based on state garrison towns, known as *trelleborgs*. Sven's raids were carefully coordinated, designed to strike multiple locations around the English coast simultaneously in order to overload the defences. Their initial purpose was not mere plunder but the far more dependable levying of *danegeld*. Fortuitously, in Aethelred the Unready, Sven had a thoroughly incapable opponent who hamstrung his own defences by forsaking the traditional duty of an Anglo-Saxon king to lead his troops in battle, resulting in a piecemeal and ineffective response. He was, moreover, willing to pay vast quantities of *danegeld* which crippled his economy and emboldened his enemy - £10,000 in 991 rising to £25,000 by 1002 and a staggering £85,000 by 1018[75].

A hoard of hacked silver and pennies of Aethelred the Unready given as *danegeld* and now in Harrogate Museum, Yorkshire. More of Athelred's coins have been found in Denmark than England, such was the tribute he paid.

---

[75] Cited in Richards (1991) p. 24

Sven may have sowed terror throughout England in the manner of his pagan ancestors, but as the strategist at the heart of a national offensive he was infinitely more calculating. He was also a Christian king who somehow reconciled the despoliation of English religious sites by his raiders with a systematic programme of church building in Scandinavia. By the turn of the first millennia, Sven's raids were moving inland into the heartland of England as this description of his actions in the year 1003 illustrates:

'This year was Exeter demolished, through the French churl Hugh, whom the lady [Aethelred's queen Emma of Normandy] had appointed her steward there. And the army destroyed the town withal, and took there much spoil. In the same year came the army up into Wiltshire. Then was collected a very great force, from Wiltshire and from Hampshire; which was soon ready on their march against the enemy: and *Earldoman* Elfric should have led them on; but he brought forth his old tricks, and as soon as they were so near, that either army looked on the other, then he pretended sickness, and began to retch, saying he was sick; and so betrayed the people that he should have led: as it is said, "When the leader is sick the whole army is hindered." When Sven saw that they were not ready, and that they all retreated, then led he his army into Wilton; and they plundered and burned the town. Then went he to Sarum; and thence back to the sea, where he knew his ships were'[76].

No nation could withstand this punishment *ad infinitum*, and it seems likely that Sven's combination of terror and economic warfare would have ultimately delivered England into his hands. Aethelred made this a certainty in 1002 however by his decision to unleash a pogrom of the innocent Scandinavian population of England, the St Brides' Day massacre. Whether the story circulated by 13th century historian John of Wendover[77] that Sven's sister Gunhilde was amongst the slain is true or not, the atrocity placed an obligation on Forkbeard, as the senior Scandinavian ruler, to avenge his kinsmen in accordance with the concept of blood-feud accepted by both English and Scandinavian society. Increasingly isolated from reality,

---

[76] *Anglo-Saxon Chronicle* entry for the year 1003 E.H.D. Vol. 1
[77] Ed. Vaughan R. *The Chronicle Attributed to John of Wallingford* (London, 1958)

Aethelred's authority essentially collapsed after the St Bride's Day massacre, although he would limp on as titular king until 1016. As a result our study of the development of the early medieval English nation state comes to an abrupt end in 1002.

For the sake of completeness however, brief mention should be made of the climax of the Viking invasion. In 1013 Aethelred fled abroad and his exhausted countrymen invited Sven to be their king. A period of confusion caused by mortality amongst the Scandinavian and English royal families followed – Sven died in 1014, enabling Aethelred to return briefly until his death in 1016, whereupon both men's heirs, Canute and Edmund Ironside, fought each other to a stalemate and agreed to partition England. By the end of 1016 Edmund too had died, leaving Canute as the first undisputed Danish king of England.

Legacy

Canute ruled with a remarkably light touch. In 1018 he promised to govern in accordance with the common law code of Edgar, last undisputed Cerdicynn king. Structurally too, England remained intact, with its shires and burghs and its *earldomen* who now kept the peace and raised taxes on Canute's behalf. Canute's astute marriage to Aethelred's widow, Emma of Normandy, also helped this programme of conciliation. The king did however install a layer of regional government, loyal Scandinavian nobles, known as *eorls* who could supervise the loyalties of the English. This cooperation with the native elite was a tremendous success; within a few years Canute's authority was virtually unchallenged, and the English economy, ravaged by nearly forty years of raiding by the king's father, experienced something of a golden age. Unified under Canute's rule, Scandinavia and England were essentially run under an early form of customs union and the lucrative North Sea trade that had so enriched the old Viking Kingdom of York a century earlier now benefitted the entire country.

When Canute died in 1035 essentially he bequeathed a country with

Danish leadership, but otherwise a politically and culturally intact English nation state. The country remained in a curious state of limbo for the next 31 years, during which several futures were open to it. One of these was Anglo-Scandinavian, despite the untimely death of Canute's heirs Harthacanute and Harold Harefoot within five year of their father. Although temporarily eclipsed by the usurpation of the throne by the last Cerdicynn king, Edward the Confessor in 1040, the latter's failure to provide an heir meant that on his death in 1066 the road to a Danish restoration was apparently open once more. This prompted Harald Hadrada, King of Norway, to launch one last great invasion of England. The prospect of a renewal of the Anglo-Scandinavian economic sphere dangled tantalisingly for a few months before the death of Hadrada and his English opponent, Harold Godwinson, within days of each other paved the way for the accession of a Norman, William the Conqueror. Though himself of Viking descent, William would ensure that it was to continental Europe that England looked for trade and expansion, not Scandinavia.

Owing to the Norman victory, little of the structure of Viking government in England survived long term, save the lingering local government institution of the *wapentake* in the north. Superficially, post Norman Conquest, the legacy of 250 years of violence, cultural assimilation, conquest and reconquest was extremely limited. Other than some place and personal names, the Danish and Norse languages apparently died out by the 13th century. Certainly Norman monarchs were not interested in preserving the distinct legal identity of the Danelaw, respected by the Cerdicynns, the land of which was subsumed under the universal Norman feudal system. Only in the periphery of the British Isles did a substantial Viking political presence endure – the Orkney islands remained under their control until at least 1266; the Scottish western Isles were not assimilated into mainstream Scottish rule until the 14th century; the Irish colony of Dublin until the 12th and the Isle of Man until 1290. Hence elements of Norse institutions there persist to the present day, including the open air parliament, the *Tynwald*.

However a more substantial Viking legacy can be discerned incorporated within the enduring structure of the English nation state. Linguistically, assimilated words within English survive to the present - s*kill*, *enthralled*, and *anger*. More subtly, a large proportion of the current English population have Scandinavian genes, particularly in the north east. Elements of Scandinavian structures survive too, particularly within the legal context that the Vikings excelled at, such as the institution of a public investigator into a violation of legal rights – the *ombudsman*.

The single most profound legacy of the Vikings in England was, however, indirect – namely the development of the nation state itself. The unintentional consequences of the Viking extinction of every English kingdom, except Wessex, cleared the field for Alfred and his successors to institute their programme of nation building. It is surely no coincidence that prior to the Viking conquests, the English kingdoms were a disparate, frequently feuding multiplicity, typical of their contemporaries in Europe. Following the successful containment of the Viking menace, emboldened by victory and united under one man's untrammelled vision, they were knitted together into the world's first nation state within thirty years.

Historiography

Medieval

The Anglo-Saxon Chronicle
Asser's Life of Alfred
Scandinavian skaldic poetry from 965 onwards, our best source is the compilation put together by Danish historian Saxo Grammaticus writing in 1200.

Current debate

Gwyn Jones [78] presents the classic defence of the early medieval Scandinavians, arguing that the term 'Viking' is an unhelpful in that it perpetuates the medieval myth that these people were simply heathen plunderers, a blight on Christian civilisation. Rather, he argues, the raiding tendencies of the Scandinavians should be viewed as an unexceptional reaction to economic and political changes in their homeland paralleled, for instance, by the predatory tendencies of the larger English kingdoms, such as Mercia against their smaller neighbours in the centuries prior to the Viking age.

HR Loyn [79] believes the Vikings were fundamentally armed traders, not colonists and that most of their invasions were based on a desire to establish an ever expanding network of trading bases, such as Dublin and York. The arrival of substantial numbers of agrarian settlers in eastern England in the late 9th century was, therefore, exceptional behaviour, exploiting the power vacuum that resulted from a civil war in Northumbria.

Dawn Hadley [80] points to the apparently rapid assimilation of Scandinavian immigrants into mainstream English society as evidence that the two cultures

---

[78] Jones (1975)
[79] Loyn (1977)
[80] Hadley D. The Vikings in England: Settlement, Society and Culture (Manchester University Press, 2007)

were in fact far more similar to each other than has previously been supposed. Contemporary English, she suggests, viewed the Scandinavians less as alien invaders, more as long lost cousins.

Benjamin Hudson[81] and Clare Downham[82] dispute the concept of a Viking conquest of Northumbria under the Ragnarssons. They argue that the latter's rule was mainly concentrated around York and that their 'Danelaw' was just one of at least two successor kingdoms that emerged following the collapse of Northumbria into civil war in the 870s. Downham believes that the national publicity which accompanied the death of Eadwulf, Lord of Bamburgh, in 913 suggests that he was a *de facto* king of at least equal status to Halfdan Ragnarsson. Hudson goes further, arguing that Eadwulf was in fact ruler of most of Northumbria during the so-called period of Viking ascendency.

Questions to consider

- Account for the success of Viking incursions into Britain before 871.

- 'The Vikings brought little but destruction to English society.' How valid is this judgement up to 871?

- To what extent was the success of Viking invasions up to 871 the result of strong leadership?

- Why did the Vikings fail to conquer Wessex?

---

[81] Hudson B. *Viking Pirates and Christian Princes: Dynasty, Religion and Empire in the North Atlantic* (Oxford University Press 2007)
[82] Downham C. *Viking Kings of Britain and Ireland: The Dynasty of Ívarr to A.D. 1014* (Edinburgh, 2007)

Chapter 7: Wessex the survivor state

Cerdicynn dynasty kings of Wessex during the Viking crisis

Egbert 802-839: Becomes *bretwalda* after defeating Mercia, creates 'buffer zone' of subject states around Wessex (Cornwall, Kent, Sussex, Essex and Surrey)

Aethelwulf 839-858: Split inheritance, gave western provinces to Athelstan

Aethelstan 839-855: ruler of Kent, Essex, Surrey and Sussex 'buffer zone' killed by Vikings (?)

Aethelbald 856-860: Seizes Wessex from Aethelwulf, father retreats to rule western 'buffer zone' for last two years of life

Ethelbert 860-865: Unified his realm into 'greater Wessex' to improve defences against the Vikings

Aethelred 865-871: Ruled in cooperation with Alfred, killed at the Battle of Merton

Alfred 'the Great' 871-899: Decisively defeats the Vikings, first king of 'all the English'.

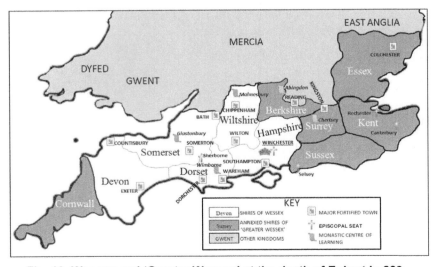

Fig. 10: Wessex and 'Greater Wessex' at the death of Egbert in 839

The strengths of Wessex

Alone of the heptarchic states, Wessex survived the Viking onslaught of the 9th century to emerge at the end as the core of a new unified state – 'England'. Whilst much of the credit for this remarkable success must be given to the architect of this state Alfred, a king of exceptional astuteness and vision, it clearly did not take place in isolation. Alfred's victory built upon foundations laid down by his predecessors which had transformed Wessex from a fragile, half formed kingdom into a uniquely efficient, militarised state by the time he ascended to the throne in 871.

Cerdic Woden-born, a Saxon prince the royal family of Wessex claimed descent from, hence Cerdicynn. from cartographer John Speed's 17th century illustration.

Wessex was the last of the heptarchic kingdoms to emerge as a fully fledged state. Its western provinces, or *scirs,* of Somerset and Devon were not conquered from the Celtic Britons until the reign of Cenwealh in the mid 7th century. The comparatively late adoption of Christianity as the state religion of Wessex towards the end of the 7th century may also have hampered Wessex's political development, as it initially deprived her kings, the Cerdicynn dynasty, of the educated monks which formed the core of the government of Northumbria, Kent and Mercia. On the plus side the longer duration of pagan rule meant that Germanic representative institutions that had disappeared in the wake of Catholic driven Roman styles of rule in the other kingdoms endured in Wessex. For example the yearly *folkmoot* at which subjects could freely air their grievances to their *earldomen* and the exceptionally powerful council of nobles, the *witangameot.* In turn the *witangameot* exercised supreme power over royal succession, which meant that the Wessex monarchy retained an unusual degree of accountability and thus loyalty from its subjects. This peculiarity would prove crucial to its survival in the period of Viking invasion.

Strategically too, once it was fully unified, Wessex occupied an exceptionally strong position. Its land borders were shorter than Mercia's, and only Mercia possessed the necessary strength to invade her. Her other neighbours, Celtic Cornwall, English Sussex and the disputed territory of Surrey (occupied variously by Kent, Mercia and Wessex), were materially weak, politically divided kingdoms who served as buffers between the Wessex heartlands and potential aggressors. Agriculturally too, Wessex possessed the most fertile land in the heptarchy, centred on Wiltshire's Salisbury plain, meaning that she could maintain the largest population and with it the largest tax base. Wessex's long, southern coastline was also richly endowed with harbours enabling lucrative trading links to develop. Uniquely for the period, the Wessex monarchy seems to have sponsored the creation of a new port to promote trade - Hamtun (now Southampton). The unusual Scandinavian style of excavated buildings here hints at long range trading links, probably the export of hides judging from the huge numbers of animal bones found on the site.[83] Finally geographically, Wessex was exceptionally well endowed with defensive positions, such as the South Downs, and, crucially, the marshes of Somerset, from which she could defy or seek sanctuary from potential aggressors.

The Downs, a range of hills along the south eastern borders of Wessex offering a natural line of defence.

The laws of King Ine (688-694) indicate that as early as the late 7th century, Wessex's government was moving in a new, more sophisticated direction than any of its predecessors. The first piece of evidence is the reference to 'shire courts' presided over by 'shiremen': 'If any man asks for justice in the presence of any *shireman*... and does not obtain it, and [the

---

[83] Holdsworth P. 'Saxon Southampton; a New Review' in proceedings of Southampton Archaeological Research Committee (1975) p.39

accused] will not give him a pledge, he [the accused] is to pay 30 shillings compensation, and within seven days make him entitled to justice'[84]. Ine, or one of his near contemporaries divided Wessex into the first 'shires' - Hampshire, Wiltshire, Devon, Dorset and Somerset and in so doing introduced possibly the single most significant revolution in local government in English history.[85]

Shires were larger and more regular in size than the irregular *scirs* of the rest of the heptarchy and were placed under the governance of royally appointed *earldomen* and *shiremen,* with clear responsibilities for governance. (Defence and tax raising were controlled by *earldomen*, justice by *shiremen*) Hence a uniform system of accountability was created between local and central government. Moreover, in another fortuitous survival from the Germanic past, *geographic* shires were ingeniously subdivided into *demographic* hundreds – each being the amount of land a hundred families required to feed themselves - under the control of a *hundredman*. This created a uniquely flexible and accountable system of governance in which the West Saxon free peasant or *ceorl* at the bottom end of the social hierarchy was only four removes from the king at the top. This regularity and simplicity made 'top down' processes, such as taxation and raising the militia, more efficient and provided some sense of consensual, fair governance – a *ceorl* in Wessex had the unique right of appeal against even his mightiest neighbour by virtue of the yearly *folkmoot* presided over by the ealdorman, or on occasion the king himself. Moreover any man brought to trial within the shire system was to an extent protected from arbitrary justice by the regularised system of courts with clear lines of authority – minor offences to be tried in the hundred court by the *hundredman*, more serious offences by the *shireman* in the shire court, with both allowing for the right of appeal to the king. Perhaps more than any other feature of the kingdom of Wessex, the shire system created strong government which inspired mutual bonds of loyalty from the top to the bottom of society. In the reigns of Egbert and Athelwulf the newly

---

[84] *The Laws of Ine* Article 8 in E.H.D. Vol. 1 (32) p.400
[85] Stubbs W. *The Constitutional History of England: Its Origins and Development* (Oxford, 1903) pp.110-111

absorbed lands of Cornwall, Berkshire, Sussex, Kent and Essex were simply turned into shires along the same model as the existing ones in the heartland of Wessex. Alfred and his successors would eventually extend this 'shiring' to the whole of the future land of England, most of which survives to the present in the form of counties.

Ine's code also upholds the Anglo-Saxon system of compensation known as *weregild,* championed by the Church as an alternative to the more traditional bloodfeud. Like the earlier codes that survive from Kent, Ine's code clearly differentiates between compensation owed to different ranks of society such as slaves, *ceorls* and ealdormen and thus helps reinforce hierarchy and status within society. It does, however, take the process further, crucially fostering a degree of social harmony by granting rights to the recently conquered Celtic inhabitants of Cornwall as well as their English conquerors, to whom it refers as 'Welsh' e.g. 'a Welshman, if he has five hides, is a man of six hundred weregild'[86]. Moreover, the commercial acumen of the Wessex dynasty, apparent in their decision to create a new port at Hamtun, is also evinced in articles designed to promote peaceful trade and the upholding of commercial contracts e.g. 'If a trader buys amongst the people in the countryside, he is to do it before witnesses.'[87]

Shifting patterns of land ownership provide a final instance of the developing resilience of Wessex. Prior to the 8th century, the standard method of land endowment by English kings had been *folkland*. This was a charter of ownership, akin to a lifelong rent which had to be renewed by the king on the death of an individual. By the turn of the 9th century land granted in perpetuity, *bookland*, had ceased to be solely the preserve of lands granted to the Church and was becoming a standard means by which the king might reward his faithful subjects. Not only did this give the king extra leverage in compelling obedience, but in granting land to a man and his successors, he was encouraging individuals to improve the agricultural yields of the land and thereby its taxable income. It also gave him a greater vested interest in

---

[86] *The Laws of Ine* Article 24.2 8. p.401
[87] Ibid. Article 25.

fighting in its defence. That the kings of Wessex were fully aware of this effect can be seen in Alfred's preface to his translation of St Augustine in the 890s, 'Every man desires that, after he has built a cottage on his lord's *folkland* and with his lord's help, he may sometimes rest himself therein... until such time as he shall earn *bookland* and an everlasting heritage through his lord's kindness'.[88]

The kings of Wessex were not the sole beneficiaries of the new ties of loyalty inspired by the *bookland* revolution. The benefits appear to have spread evenly across the heptarchy. However, when it is viewed as a development alongside that of Ine's law codes designed to promote commerce and Wessex's shire system that emphasised the accountability of royal government to its people, its benefits combined to create an overall sense of social cohesion and loyalty within the heartland of Wessex quite unlike anywhere else in the heptarchy. This accumulative effect would be exploited successfully by Alfred the Great, both its beneficiary and the visionary who would use it as a basis for nation building.

Egbert's consolidation 802-839

Unlike the other kingdoms of southern Britain, Wessex was never overrun by Mercia in the 8th century, although Offa had enjoyed a brief period of political domination in the 780s when he sponsored the successful candidate for the throne, Beorhtric, during a brief civil war between rival claimants (*aethlings*). Charlemagne's decision to offer a refuge in France to the loser, Egbert, ensured the long term independence of Wessex. After the death of Beorhtric in 802, Charlemagne's support enabled Egbert to seize the throne of Wessex, from which he would

A Victorian engraving of Egbert.

---

[88] Alfred, Preface to his translation of Augustine's *Soliloques* in Ed. *Asser's Life of Alfred and other sources* (London, 2004) p.139

pursue a policy of aggressive independence, culminating in his victory over Mercia at the battle of Ellendun in 825.

Egbert followed up Ellendun by leading a confederation of all Mercia's former colonies in an invasion that culminated in total conquest by 829. The submission of Northumbria to his overlordship by the end of that year marked a remarkable turnaround which saw Egbert emerge as a *bretwalda* as strong as Offa before him. Although Egbert subsequently lost control of Mercia the following year, Wessex retained her supremacy in the heptarchy for the remainder of the 9th century.

The former colonies of Mercia may have hoped that Egbert's victory would free them from conquest, but with the sole exception of distant East Anglia, they were disappointed. Sussex, Essex and Kent were united under Wessex overlordship even more intense than that of Offa's Mercia. It was not mere imperial governance that was Egbert's intention, but political absorption into a 'Greater Wessex' – the royal families of each were entirely dispossessed and replaced by Cerdicynns[89] – Kent, in particular, appears to have served as an apprentice realm for the king's preferred heir to learn the craft of kingship. In 838 Egbert completed his conquest of the south at the battle of Hingston Down by destroying the last independent Cornish army. His realm of 'Greater Wessex' was complete. Not only did this enlarged kingdom greatly expand the prestige of the Wessex monarchy, (the incorporation of the formerly Kentish Archdiocese of Canterbury was of particular significance here) but it also meant that the east, west and north east of Wessex's heartlands were protected by swathes of friendly territory. Whether this was a deliberate strategy of securing buffer zones around his realm, or mere opportunism is unclear, but either way Egbert's conquests would prove vital to his grandson Alfred's ultimate victory over the Viking invasion later in the 9th century.

---

[89] Although the *earldomen* below them remained the same and indeed were rewarded with more land in Wessex herself thereby creating dynastic links between the formally separate realms.

Facing up to the Vikings 839-870

Egbert's son and successor, Athelwulf, and his five grandsons' reigns were increasingly dominated by the growing threat of Viking raids and, from 870 onwards, actual invasion. Their focus perforce was consolidation therefore, as opposed to the further expansion of Wessex power. The only exception to this was Aethelwulf's seizure of Berkshire off Mercia in 851, adding a much needed further buffer zone to Wessex and providing a measure of security over the Thames valley – the standard invasion route for Vikings advancing from the north east.

Aethelwulf was no more than an adequate king whose unique legacy was to sire no less than five sons as potential *aethlings*. Unsurprisingly this led to fratricidal squabbling, compounded by Aethelwulf's two long periods of absence from his realm, one to wage war in Wales in 853 and the second to accompany his youngest son Alfred on a pilgrimage to Rome in 855. In his absence his eldest son and favoured *atheling,* Aethelstan, appears to have been killed fighting Viking raiders off the coast of Kent. The oldest surviving brother, Aethelbald, pre-empted a succession crisis by seizing the government of Wessex in a coup in 856. Aethelwulf appears to have accepted this as a *fait accompli* and gone into internal exile, ruling the eastern provinces of Wessex; Kent, Sussex, Surrey and Essex; and leaving the heartlands to Aethelbald, until he died in 858.

After Athelwulf's death the schism in the realm of Wessex continued when the *witangameot* refused to let Aethelbald succeed to the eastern half of Greater Wessex, awarding it instead to the next eldest brother Ethelbert. Aethelbald, moreover, created scandal by marrying his widowed stepmother, the Carolingian princess, Judith. Although he died within two years of his father in 860, the damage to the realm had been done: A political fault line had been opened up between the eastern and western halves of the Cerdicynn's realms at exactly the moment when they needed to unite. Ethelbert was granted dominion over the entire realm on his brother's death, but was still trying to reconcile the two halves when between 860 and 864 a powerful Viking raiding force arrived. Taking advantage of Wessex's lack of cohesion, the raiders swiftly ransacked the principle port of Hamtun and Wessex's capital, Winchester. The raiders were subsequently defeated by the combined forces of Hampshire and Berkshire. But, nonetheless, this event sent a clear signal to the Vikings. If the English could not even defend the capital of their greatest kingdom then they were ripe not just for raiding but for conquest. Accordingly, in 866 the Viking Great Heathen Army landed in East Anglia and began a campaign to subjugate the whole of Britain to pagan Scandinavian rule.

Between 866 and 870 the Great Heathen Army unleashed a remarkable campaign of conquest and rapine across northern and eastern England. Forcing a peace on the timid king of East Anglia, Edmund, they were able to use his lands as a base for a rapid invasion of Northumbria, which fell within weeks. An incursion into Mercia followed, whose king Burghred appealed to Wessex for support. King Ethelberth of Wessex had died in 865, clearing the throne for the altogether more redoubtable Aethelred, who with his sole surviving brother, now *aethling* Alfred, would form the only effective resistance to the Vikings during the 860s. Unfortunately, Aethelred was not given the chance to show his military talents. He managed to trap the Great Heathen Army in Leicester and place it under joint Mercian-West Saxon siege, but the weak and thoroughly intimidated Burghred squandered this one chance to end the Viking threat and negotiated a truce which allowed the Great Heathen Army to retire to York unharmed.

The Vikings then proceeded to bleed Mercian finances dry in the form of *danegeld* tribute, exacted in return for a pledge not to invade again from their new colony of Northumbria. The West Saxons withdrew in disgust, leaving Burghred to pay such exorbitant sums that his government subsequently collapsed in 973. Burghred entered into exile in Rome and the Vikings were able to seize most of Mercia without a fight. With Northumbria occupied and Mercia prostrate, the West Saxons were unable to provide effective support to the last remaining English kingdom to the north of them, East Anglia. In 870 it, plus the West Saxon province of Essex, were both overrun. By the end of that year Wessex was all that remained between the Vikings and a total conquest of the English people. Its ranks thickened by reinforcements from Scandinavia, the Great Heathen Army marched south towards the borders of Wessex in December 870.

871: The year of battles

871 AD must surely rank as one of the most appallingly violent years in British history. Laconic contemporary accounts only provide a glimpse into the full horror of this year in which the West Saxons and Vikings fought each other to a bloody standstill, having engaged in no less than six pitched battles and innumerable skirmishes within twelve months. The *Anglo-Saxon Chronicle* simply states 'there was much slaughter on either hand' but that at in the end 'the Danes had possession of the place of slaughter'[90].

This bloodshed reflects the stalemate that had emerged along the Wessex border. Having forced Burghred of Mercia into exile, the Viking Great Heathen Army was able to concentrate all its resources on the invasion of Wessex, by now the sole remaining independent English state. The Vikings comprised a very mobile, largely mounted and well equipped force of experienced warriors which the balance of current opinion puts at between two and four thousand strong, buoyed up by repeated victories over the rest of the heptarchy and greedy for land and plunder. On the debit side, its leadership was neither as united nor as bold as it had been, owing to the death or departure of its inspiration commander, Ivar the Boneless, after the conquest of East Anglia in 870. Command was now shared by two Danish kings, Guthrum and Bagsaec, who were much more cautious and unimaginative in their approach. Accordingly, their invasion of Wessex at the start of 871 was both slow and predictable, following the line of the Thames valley towards Reading. The armed forces of Wessex were thus given adequate warning to mobilise fully in response.

---

[90] *Anglo-Saxon Chronicle* entry for 871 in E.H.D. Vol. 1

The army of Wessex was theoretically the same in composition and command as those of Northumbria, Mercia and East Anglia, all of whom had failed abysmally in the face of the Viking threat. Like them, it comprised a part time peasant militia, the *fyrd*, built around a core of nobles and their small retinue of professional soldiers or *hearthweru* (literally "hearth warriors"). Typically only the latter were mounted and equipped to the same standard as the Vikings, and smaller, more mobile contingents of the latter had repeatedly triumphed in the years running up to 871 by outmanoeuvring their slow moving opponents and defeating them piecemeal before they could combine. The efficient shire system of local government meant that the *fyrd* of Wessex could be assembled more quickly in ready-made 'divisions', under the command of each shire's ealdorman, compared to the other English kingdoms. Moreover, unimaginative tactics by the Viking leaders plus the geographical limitations imposed by the hilly terrain of northern Wessex negated their advantage and Wessex was able to gather substantial armies which at least matched and probably outnumbered their enemy throughout the 871 campaign.

The comparatively large population of Wessex also allowed for an exceptionally large *fyrd*, and probably an unusually large core of *hearthweru,* given the greater tax base that the kings of Wessex could call upon. The army of Wessex was thus able to fight harder and make good its losses more effectively than any of its contemporaries. Finally, the army Wessex was blessed with very effective leadership – divisional commanders such as Aethelwulf, *Earldoman* of Berkshire, being capable of fighting and winning small battles on their own, as well as effectively incorporating their shire army into a larger, national force. High command was just as solid – King Aethelred was a capable and determined commander,

A young *aethling* Alfred leads the West Saxons to victory at Ashdown in 871 in a woodcut by Morris Meredith Williams from 1913. Physically frail, Alfred was an unlikely warrior king but his bravery is uncontestable.

whilst his sole surviving brother, the *aethling* Alfred, proved an effective deputy. Furthermore, perhaps by virtue of the unique tradition of accountable monarchy in Wessex, her inhabitants seem to have been willing to fight for longer and endure worse privations than they would for the rest of the heptarchy.

This combination therefore, of a Viking army of unprecedented size and experience facing a large, inexperienced, but resolute West Saxon force led to a brutal and prolonged confrontation. It began when the Great Heathen Army crossed the borders of north Wessex at the end of 870 and wintered in Reading. The *Anglo-Saxon Chronicle* provides a chronological account of the battles which followed and the commanders who were killed by both sides:

- *Englefield, 31st December 870 – 1st January 871 (Wessex victory)*: A surprise attack by *Earldoman* Aethelwulf and the *fyrd* of Berkshire defeated a Viking army heading south from Reading resulting in the death of *Jarl* Sidroc.

- *First Battle of Reading, 4th January 871 (Viking victory)*: A combined attack on Reading by the royal army under King Aethelred and the Berkshire *fyrd* under Aethelwulf was bloodily repulsed. Aethelwulf was killed.

- *Ashdown, 8th January 871 (Wessex victory)*: A pre-emptive attack on the Viking advancing out of Reading before it had formed up by *atheling* Alfred resulted in the greatest victory Wessex would enjoy in 871. Viking King Bagsaec was killed as were his Jarls, Sidroc the Elder, Sidroc the Younger, Osbern, Fraena and Harald and the Great Heathen Army retreated back to Reading for a second time. Alfred earned the title 'the Wild Boar of Ashdown' for his exploits.

- *Basing, 22nd January 871 (Viking victory)*: A third Viking advance out of Reading now under the sole command of Guthrum was engaged by the main army of Wessex under Aethelred and the latter was defeated and compelled to retire. The Viking advance into Wessex continued. However losses on Wessex's side cannot have been too great; no commanders are listed as having been killed and within two months Aethelred was able to initiate battle again.

- *Merton 22 March 871 (Viking victory):* After two months of raiding, the Great Heathen Army was engaged at Merton in Wiltshire. This was a disastrous battle for Wessex whose army clearly lost heavily. One of its commanders, Bishop Heahmund, was killed and most importantly Aethelred himself was mortally injured, dying a few days later.

- *Wilton, unknown date in May (Viking victory):* The defeat at Basing had such a devastating effect on Wessex that she was unable to counter the great Heathen Army's progress for nearly two months, during which time it pillaged its way through the heart of the kingdom and had almost reached the south coast when it was finally confronted by the main Wessex army, now under the command of Alfred. In this, his first battle as king, Alfred lost again and by this point his resources were exhausted. Finally at this point, as the *Chronicle* records, 'The West Saxons made peace with the raiding army'.[91]

Alfred's coronation – staring into the precipice?

Alfred's truce with Guthrum after Wilton was a punitive one. The already strained Wessex treasury was required to hand over substantial *danegeld* as a token of defeat. Indeed, a record of four defeats in six battles at first sight looks like humiliating failure. However, the mere fact that Wessex had been able to *survive* six successive battles against an exceptionally large and experienced Viking army, and be in a position to negotiate afterwards, set it apart from the other states in the heptarchy in terms of its resources and its will to fight. Moreover, the ferocity of West Saxon resistance had shaken the

---

[91] Ibid.

Vikings and inflicted very severe losses on their finite pool of experienced warriors. As a consequence the years 872-875 saw the Great Heathen Army swing north and east away from Wessex to destroy remaining resistance in already ravaged Mercia and East Anglia. This distraction bought Wessex and her new king Alfred, hurriedly crowned between the battles of Merton and Wilton, desperately needed breathing space. Had the Great Heathen Army pressed home its attack into 872 it is likely that Wessex would have been rendered prostrate and forced to surrender – contemporary writers agree that the defeat at Wilton used up all the remaining resources in manpower and resolve of Wessex. Alfred's biographer, Asser, is more dramatic, punctuating a usually dispassionate account with this vivid description of the outcome of 871: 'The Saxons were virtually annihilated to a man in this single year in eight battles against the Vikings in which one Viking king and nine earls, with countless men, were killed, leaving aside the innumerable skirmishes by day and night... How many thousands of the Viking army is not known, except to God alone'.[92]

Setting aside Asser's poetic license, it is clear that Alfred had inherited a kingdom in the last stage of desperation. The six battles of 871 had traumatised and drained the kingdom of resources and had only succeeded in fighting the Vikings to a standstill. Never has an English king, before or since, inherited a kingdom on the brink of such catastrophe. Viewed from this perspective, Alfred's achievements then in the three decades that followed, impressive in their own right, represent one of the most remarkable reversals of fortune in history.

---

[92] Asser *Life of King Alfred* in Ed. Keynes S. and Lapidge M. (London, 2004) p. 81

Historiography

Medieval:

The Anglo Saxon Chronicle

Current debate:

Richard Abels in *Alfred the Great: War, Kingship and Culture in Anglo-Saxon England* (Pearson, Harlow, 1998) p.285 believes that although its greater wealth and the stoic qualities of Egbert, Aethelwulf and his sons led to protracted resistance, in essence Wessex was no less vulnerable than the rest of the heptarchic kingdoms to Viking invasion. It was the unique qualities of Alfred therefore that ensured Wessex's survival.

David Starkey in *The Monarchy of England Volume 1: Beginnings* (Chatto and Windus, London, 2004) p.50 does not deny the pivotal contribution of Alfred in ensuring Wessex's survival, but he does credit Alfred's predecessors with a greater role in bringing this about, arguing for the 'uniqueness' of Wessex. In particular, Egbert is credited with raising Wessex to the status of the dominant power in Britain in the years immediately preceding the Viking invasions and bequeathing both an army and a system of government which was uniquely efficient and consensual and therefore better able to counter the Viking threat.

Sir Frank Stenton in *Anglo-Saxon England* (Oxford University Press, 1971) p.235 agrees with Starkey's opinion that Egbert's legacy was pivotal in ensuring Wessex's survival, although he emphasises the importance of the conquest of Wessex's neighbours and their use as 'buffer states' to blunt the Viking invasion. He does concede, however, that though this conquest bought time for Wessex, the kingdom would not have ultimately survived without the unique contribution of Alfred.

Questions to consider

- How is the emergence of Wessex as the dominant power in England up to 871 best explained?

- To what extent was 9th century Wessex different from the other Anglo-Saxon kingdoms?

- What best explains the survival of Wessex in the face of Viking invasion up to 871?

- 'A conqueror but little else.' How valid is this judgement of Egbert?

- 'The kings of Wessex between the death of Egbert and the accession of Alfred accomplished little'. Discuss.

Chapter 8: Alfred: Father of England?

Key events in Alfred's reign

866: Alfred becomes heir apparent to his sole surviving brother Aethelred.

870-71: 'The Year of Battles' – Alfred wins a military reputation after victory at Ashdown, and in April 871 is crowned king following the death of Aethelred.

871-878: Viking pressure grows on Wessex, Alfred is forced to buy them off through tribute or 'Danegeld'. Alfred is criticised after trapping the Viking leader Guthrum at Wareham then letting him go again.

Early 878: Guthrum launches a strike on Alfred himself at Chippenham, the King and his family only just escape. They flee to Athelney in the Somerset marshes whilst the Vikings begin to occupy Wessex. Alfred sends out spies to try and rebuild the English army.

Late 878: Alfred rallies his troops on the border of Somerset and Wiltshire at Egbert's Stone. He marches on Guthrum and defats him in battle at Edington. The Treaty of Wedmore which follows forces Christian baptism on Guthrum as the price of survival and expels his followers to East Anglia. For the first time 'the English' are mentioned as a single people with Alfred as their King.

878-885: Alfred establishes control over all of the southern parts of Britain which he now calls England. He builds fortified towns or *burghs* to defend them, reforms the army and founds the Royal Navy.

886: Alfred's army seizes Viking occupied London.

888: Alfred releases his *Doom Book*, the first universal English law code.

892-7: The Vikings resume their assault but Alfred's defences hold, in the end they retreat to the Viking controlled north.

897-9: Alfred retires from ruling, his son Edward the Elder and his daughter Aethelflead, Lady of the Mercians and son-in-law Aethelred of Mercia, take over. He devotes his last years to translating Latin texts into English for the benefit of his subjects.

899: Alfred dies. Edward is crowned King of England.

871-878: The parable of the cakes

The parable of Alfred and the cakes from a mid-20th century children's book.

The first phase of Alfred's reign was undistinguished, characterised by a tendency on the part of the inexperienced king to let opportunities slip through his fingers. Granted, the Wessex that Alfred inherited in 871 was a kingdom in desperate straits, assailed by enemies, bloodied by frequent battle and impoverished by plunder and the payment of *danegeld*. Nonetheless, the king was presented with an opportunity to consolidate and refresh the still formidable defences of Wessex during the next five years as, during this period, Viking attention was focussed on consolidating their conquest of Northumbria and eastern Mercia.

Alfred did remarkably little; indeed his sole achievement of note appears to have been currency reform aimed at enriching the silver content of the West Saxon penny. As a consequence, when Guthrum's Viking army renewed the offensive against Wessex in 876, the kingdom was no better prepared than it had been during the last attack of 870-71. A lightning strike by Guthrum from Reading cut diagonally through Wessex into Dorset, pillaging and spreading terror as it went. However, expected support from a Viking fleet did not materialise and the Vikings were thus trapped, outnumbered within the walls of Wareham on the Dorset coast. Alfred's actions at this juncture, when he apparently had the Vikings at his mercy and let them escape are glossed over by contemporary accounts which all favour the king. The *Anglo-Saxon Chronicle* has this to say:

'And this year the army stole into Wareham, a fort of the West-Saxons. The king [Alfred] afterwards made peace with them; and they gave him as hostages those who were worthiest in the army; and swore with oaths on the holy bracelet, which they would not before to any nation, that they would readily go out of his kingdom. Then, under colour of this, their cavalry stole by night into Exeter.'[93]

Reading between the lines, it appears that Alfred naively assumed that the sacred value of an oath in Christian English society carried the same weight in pagan, Scandinavian culture. The Treaty of Wareham agreed between himself and Guthrum therefore depended for its enforcement on a shared oath taken by the two kings over the cross and a pagan 'holy bracelet'. Alfred severely underestimated the ruthlessness of Guthrum, who was prepared not only to renege on his oath, but also sacrifice his hostages. Somehow Guthrum managed to emerge from Alfred's encirclement with his army intact, and far from departing from Wessex as he had sworn, he seized Exeter, the fortified capital of Devon. Here he went to ground, once again awaiting the arrival of his invasion fleet, only retreating when the latter was destroyed in a storm off Swanage.

Alfred was lucky to survive the catastrophic Treaty of Wareham. His salvation lay in the fortuitous storm that eliminated the Viking fleet, rather than any action of his. The traditional view voiced by Alfred's biographer, Asser, is that this period was a redemptive one for Alfred, one in which he acknowledged the failings and sought to make amends: 'We may believe that the calamity was brought upon the king aforesaid, because, in the beginning of his reign, when he was a youth, and influenced by youthful feelings, he would not listen to the petitions which his subjects made to him for help in their necessities, or for relief from those who oppressed them; but he repulsed them from him, and paid no heed to their requests'.[94]

Asser states that despite his failings, Alfred's people never abandoned faith in him. The former was, however, as much a propagandist as an historian, and working, moreover, within a carefully contrived public relations campaign

---

[93] *Anglo-Saxon Chronicle* entry for the year 876 E.H.D. Vol. 1
[94] Asser *Life of King Alfred* para 66 in Ed. Keynes S. and Lapidge M. (London, 2004)

which cast Alfred as rightful king of England, ordained by God and acclaimed by his people. Any suggestion that Alfred had lost their confidence therefore would be inadmissible. However, Justin Pollard has unearthed evidence of considerable discontent from both nobles and clergy within Wessex's *witangaemot* with Alfred's policies. Indeed Pollard suggests that the leaders of this faction, Earldoman Wulfere of Wiltshire and Aethelred, Archbishop of Canterbury, had despaired of Wessex surviving as an English kingdom and had entered into secret negotiations with Guthrum regarding their positions in the event of a Viking takeover of the kingdom, possibly with a view to Wulfere taking over as puppet king of Wessex in the same manner as Ceolwulf in Mercia[95]. Pollard believes that Guthrum's raid on Alfred and his family at Chippenham in northern Wiltshire at the start of 878 was, in fact, Wulfere's plan rather than a piece of Viking opportunism. Either way by 878 Alfred's grip on Wessex was slipping rapidly.

It is to this scenario that Pollard attributes the otherwise incomprehensible perpetuation of the story of Alfred and the cakes, surely the most famous anecdote about any early medieval King.[96] The story, he reasons, is a morality parable on the model of the Gospels. Alfred, beaten and in hiding takes shelter in the cottage of a peasant woman who grants him a place at her fire on condition he minds the cakes baking upon it. The cakes symbolise Wessex, and Alfred's falling asleep and allowing them to burn is representative of the torpor like state he had exhibited during his first seven years of kingship. The peasant woman represents the righteously indignant *witangameot*; her chastisement of the neglectful king express the sentiments of no confidence that almost led to his downfall at the start of 878. Crucially, however, Alfred's somewhat meek acknowledgment of the rightfulness of his rebuke symbolises his acceptance of his failings as king, and his resolution to do better. Before he could do so, however, he would have to survive.

---

[95] Pollard *Alfred the Great: The Man who made England* (London, 2006) pp. 157-170. Tellingly, Alfred disposed Wulfere of his position as ealdorman within months of regaining his throne in 878.
[96] Ibid. pp. 176-77. Asser supports this assertion in his description of Alfred's vision of St. Neot who explains that Alfred's calamities are God's punishment for the king's neglect of his kingdom.

878: Crisis and Recovery

During the Christmas feast in the first days of 878 a flying column of Vikings left Mercian Gloucester and made for Chippenham where Alfred and his family were feasting. The flying column intended to capture and eliminate the last English king and his successors at a single stroke. They came perilously close to succeeding. Somehow Alfred learned of their endeavour and fled with a small company of followers, becoming a fugitive in his own kingdom who, the *Anglo-Saxon Chronicle* relates, 'Uneasily sought the woods and fastnesses of the moors'[97].

The Somerset Levels around Athelney, refuge of Alfred and his court. This photograph, taken during recent flooding, resembles the conditions that would have been encountered in 878.

The situation was in truth, not as desperate as it might first appear. The 'moors' that Alfred fled to were the Somerset Levels, an unassailable expanse of wetland which the king had known intimately since childhood. He established an island fortress at Athelney in the centre of the Levels, from where he could operate in safety. Moreover, the Viking forces that now attempted to overrun Wessex were insufficient for the task - many available

---

[97] *Anglo-Saxon Chronicle*, entry for the year 878 E.H.D. Vol. 1

troops having been soaked up in numerous sieges of fortified towns across the kingdom. As a result forces loyal to Alfred were still able to move around the country. In the case of *Ealdorman* Odda of Devon these forces were actually able to take the offensive, surprising and massacring the western army of Guthrum's invasion force including a Ragnarsson, Ubba, at the Battle of Countisbury.

The destruction of Ubba's army left Guthrum with a temporary shortage of men to complete the conquest of Wessex during the winter and spring of 878. He would be able to reinforce his forces from Scandinavia from late spring onwards when sailing conditions were favourable. Alfred thus had a narrow window of at most four months to regain control of his kingdom.

Alfred's most successful subordinate, Odda of Devon, was preoccupied with defending the west coast of Wessex and was thus unable to support his king. Fortuitously, the *Ealdorman* of Somerset, Aelfere, remained loyal and his *fyrd* provided Alfred with the nucleus of an army. According to Asser, Alfred spent winter and early spring 878 waging guerrilla war on the Vikings, partly to safeguard his marshland base at Athelney, but primarily perhaps for the benefit of his subjects, to remind them that their king still lived and still fought. Alfred clearly despatched messengers throughout his kingdom seeking to rally all surviving West Saxon forces to his banner. He may well have also swept up groups of armed refugees from the other English kingdoms.

Lacking a conventional supply base, Alfred faced enormous difficulties raising a sizeable army, in terms of equipping and feeding them. An archaeological dig by the B.B.C. *Time Team* series in 1994[98] suggests that he may have solved the former by establishing forges on Athelney. The food issue remained insoluble, however, meaning that, after assembling his army, Alfred would have to seek out decisive battle with Guthrum immediately or face the prospect of his army dispersing through starvation, thus severely restricting the king's strategic options before the campaign even commenced.

---

[98] B.B.C. *Time Team* Series 1 Episode 1 'The Guerrilla Base of the King' aired 16.01.94 in which a lump of slag associated with medieval iron smelting was recovered.

Even more pressing than the food situation was morale. Alfred's military record since becoming king was poor and any force he was likely to assemble would certainly be less well trained and probably smaller than Guthrum's. By virtue of his superior supply chain, Guthrum would also be able to choose when and where the two sides would meet in battle, if at all. To inspire his improvised army with a will to win in such circumstances represents an extraordinary achievement on Alfred's part. Yet he seems to have done precisely that at the local *moot* site of Egbert's Stone on the border of Somerset and Wiltshire.

The Alfred Tower, an 18th century folly built on the site of Egbert's stone, the *folkmoot* where Alfred rallied the *fyrds* of Somerset, Wiltshire and Sussex on the eve of his decisive confrontation with Guthrum's Great Heathen Army in May 878.

Asser tells us that Alfred had succeeded in gathering the *fyrds* of Somerset, Hampshire and Wiltshire (presumably minus their traitorous *ealdorman,* Wulfere). With his own *hearthweru,* plus refugee contingents from other kingdoms, his force has been estimated as numbering between 2500-4000 men, a similar size to Guthrum's, but containing far fewer experienced troops. Sadly neither the *Anglo-Saxon Chronicle* nor Asser tells us what Alfred said to his men at Egbert's Stone, only that 'They received him, as he deserved, with joy and acclamations.'[99] It would need more than joy and acclamation to defeat the Vikings, however. It was at Egbert's Stone, Starkey believes, that Alfred first made use of English nationalism to win his troops' hearts and minds. Starkey has detected a subtle but significant shift in the language of Alfred's proclamations before and after the events of 878 – Alfred is no longer 'King of the West Saxons', but 'King of all the English' – *cyning aelles angelcynnes*. He also increasingly makes use of 'we' when referring to his subjects. For the first time in history, Alfred claims the loyalty of a people by virtue of their shared kinship, traditions and sense of belonging – the hitherto disparate English peoples have been welded into one by the Viking threat and he, Alfred, by virtue of being the last free English king, lays claim to govern all of them. Nationalism, one of the greatest drivers in human history, was thus first aired at Egbert's Stone.

It was evidently successful. On a date between 5-7 May 878 Alfred's army headed north east seeking out Guthrum. The Viking king decided to offer battle and two days later the two sides met near the village of Edington in Wiltshire.

Tinhead Hill, an escarpment of Salisbury Plain overlooking the village of Edington, the most likely location for the decisive Battle of Edington fought on 5-7 May 878. Guthrum's Vikings would have formed a shield wall across the sky line whilst the photograph was taken from the likely forming up point of Alfred's West Saxon army.

---

[99] Asser para 68

Contemporary sources are disappointingly vague about the Battle of Edington, undoubtedly one of the most significant in English history. No archaeological evidence has ever been found and thus we are still unclear as to exactly where the battle was fought, although at the time of writing Edington Hill, a peninsula of the Salisbury Plain plateau seems the most plausible[100]. The stakes could not have been higher – the Vikings were presented with a unique opportunity to crush the last independent English king and with him any organised resistance to their invasion. From Alfred and his English army's perspective, Edington really was their last chance – if this army was destroyed the Viking reinforcements, due within the month, would eliminate the possibility of forming another. Moreover, the hideous fates of Aelle of Northumbria and Edmund of East Anglia must have focussed Alfred's mind as to the consequences of defeat. There is no reason therefore to doubt Asser's assertion that Alfred led his men into battle personally. He had nothing to lose. Asser has the following to say about the course of the battle itself:

'Fighting ferociously, forming a dense shield-wall against the whole army of the Pagans, and striving long and bravely...at last he [Alfred] gained the victory. He overthrew the Pagans with great slaughter, and smiting the fugitives, he pursued them as far as the fortress' [i.e., Chippenham][101].

A modern re-enactment of the Battle of Edington.

---

[100] Michael Wood believes the battle to have been fought on the flat land at the base of Salisbury Plain, Richard Abels suggests the nearby Iron Age turf fortress of Bratton Camp whilst local tradition holds that it was fought on Edington hill, a peninsula of raised ground that juts out of the Salisbury Plain massif above the village itself. From a tactical perspective, plus the fact that the other two locations have been excavated and yielded no finds, the author believes Edington hill to be the most plausible location.
[101] Asser para 68.

We will never know whether the inspiration of English nationalism or superior tactics led to victory over the Vikings, but either way by this one stroke, Alfred had transformed his fortunes and those of his infant vision of a united 'Aenglaland'. Breaking with his habitually merciful approach to the enemy, Alfred's determined pursuit and slaughter of the fleeing Vikings must have signalled to Guthrum that the King of Wessex was no longer the weak and hesitant leader he had known in the past. Besieged in Chippenham by a victorious English army baying for Viking blood, Guthrum agreed to a peace treaty exclusively on Alfred's terms.

The resulting Treaty of Wedmore represents an historic rearrangement of the political order of early medieval England. For the first time Alfred makes written use of his nationalistic title 'King of all the English' and in so states the right of the Cerdicynn family to rule not just over Wessex, but over all the English lands. So began a process that would take three generations of kings and culminate in the unification of 'Aenglaland' for the first time in its history. Shorter term, Guthrum's pledge to leave Wessex at a time of Alfred's choosing, to submit, with thirty of his leading followers, to Christian baptism and to accept Alfred as his godfather represents a clear and unequivocal gesture of subordination, the first time a Viking king had ever submitted to the authority of an English king. Perhaps overawed by the scale of Alfred's change of fortune, Guthrum made no move to renounce or evade the Treaty of Wedmore as he had the earlier Treaty of Wareham, and retired peacefully to rule East Anglia, posing no further threat to Alfred.

878-892: Back from the brink

The events of 878 clearly left their mark on Alfred. From henceforth he ruled energetically and with exceptional astuteness until his death in 899. Guthrum may have been defeated, but the Vikings still posed a threat, and Alfred knew that they would inevitably return at some point. He, therefore, spent the bulk of the remainder of his reign preparing for renewed invasion. These preparations involved mobilising the entirety of Wessex's population and resources in a systematic programme of defence, reminiscent of

Churchill's 'total war' strategy of World War Two. Alfred's already war ravaged subjects would be repeatedly and heavily taxed in terms of both wealth and labour in the pursuit of this project, and it is a testimony to the successful marketing of his vision of a united England that there were few murmurs of rebellion either in Wessex or western Mercia which essentially became Alfred's colony after he married his daughter, Aethelflaed, to the leading Mercian *Ealdorman,* Aethelred. Crucially, Alfred was able to secure papal permission to tax church estates or *bookland*, usually exempt from royal taxation, thus increasing his income by perhaps 20%.

These resources were invested in a triple tier defence system. For the first time in English history a standing navy of large longships was constructed to intercept Viking raiders at sea. A mobile standing force of *hearthweru* were maintained at Winchester at all times to act as the core of a field army. Most significant, however, was Alfred's programme of systematic *burgh* construction – a network of fortified towns that represented the largest construction project in England between the fall of the Roman Empire and the Norman Conquest of 1066. Alfred's intention was that every part of his realm should be within a day's march of a *burgh*. Their purpose was to provide a sanctuary for his subjects and their possessions and to deprive the Vikings of their mobility – an invading army would have to lay siege to every *burgh* that lay in its path or risk being cut off from its ships. The *burghs* were astutely sited to provide protection to large population centres and to obvious avenues of invasion – five lay astride the River Thames. Burghs also possessed armouries, centres of government, food supplies and a mint and thus provided centres for local defence. They were connected to each other by roads or *herepaths,* along which reinforcements could be moved. Longer term, Alfred intended that they would pay for themselves as centres of trade and he therefore granted them freedom of commerce.

Manning and supporting this network of fortifications was a prodigious effort. A document known as the *Burghal Hideage* survives explaining how it was done. Possession of land or 'hideage' by an individual automatically gave that individual fixed responsibilities towards their local burgh in terms of providing manpower to build it and to garrison it. The latter amounted to over 27,000 men at any one time, 25% of all the freemen in Wessex. A rotation system was introduced to ensure that this conscription did not prevent men from farming.

The 9th century earth ramparts of Wareham, Dorset, one of Alfred's burghs.

These three tiers represent a system of 'defence in depth' that hampered Viking advantages of speed, skill and ferocity and emphasised English advantages of superior numbers, control of lines of communication and organisation. Alfred's intention was that the defence of his realm should no longer be decided in the chancy conditions of battle, but through the relentless grinding down of the enemy via sieges.

Alfred cannot take all the credit for the success of this system; it was only possible because of the efficient shire structure of local government he had inherited. Moreover it was not an original idea; the Carolingians had already developed their own version of *burghs* on the continent in response to Viking raids – indeed Alfred may well have obtained the idea from his Carolingian mother-in-law, Judith. What was unique about Alfred's *burgh* system was its universality. When the Vikings finally invaded again in 892 their extensive probing found no weak points in Wessex' system of defence. So successful was it that Alfred's successors, Edward and Athelstan, would ultimately evolve the *burgh* system from a defensive into an offensive role and use it as the central component in their successful conquest of Viking occupied England.

Crucially, Alfred's relationship with the Vikings was not defined solely in terms of hostility. His vision of English nationalism was sufficiently broad as to incorporate peaceful Scandinavian settlers. Thus his diplomacy from the 880s onwards is focussed on separating the first generation of Vikings, settled, peaceful and increasingly Christianised, from successive waves of pagan invaders. The culmination of this policy was his boundary agreement with Guthrum in 886, wherein southern and midland England was diagonally divided into mutually recognised realms. The south and west, including Wessex, Cornwall, Sussex, Kent and Western Mercia to Alfred, the north and east to Guthrum including Essex, East Anglia and eastern Mercia, collectively known as 'the Danelaw'. This agreement lent further legitimacy to Alfred's claim to pan-English authority over lands beyond Wessex and also created a buffer zone of Danelaw Vikings who were more interested in peaceful co-existence and trade with their English neighbour than ongoing conflict.

In addition to copious revenue, Alfred's projection of himself as 'King of the English' required the careful projection of the royal image throughout he claimed to rule. 'Monetary renovation' helped address both these challenges. Again adopting a Carolingian strategy, this policy required the systematic recall of an estimated 10 million silver pennies from the disparate mints of the southern English kingdoms, their rebasement (an increase in the proportion of silver) and reissue as the first standardised English currency – a prodigious effort for an early medieval monarchy which required an expansion in the number of royal mints from two to nine. For this to be possible Alfred must have obtained large quantities of pure silver, most likely through wool trade with eastern Germany. The newly issued coinage was infinitely more stable in value than its predecessors, actively encouraging trade and facilitating tax collection. The coins also provided the most publically accessible image of the king – Alfred's penny consciously draws upon Roman designs and possesses the unambiguous inscription 'Alfred, King of the English'.

Massive military investment, fiscal reform and a conscious promotion of national unity thus turned Alfred's embryonic England into a 'total war' war kingdom, a state which, like Britain and the Soviet Union in World War Two, had geared its entire resources towards the prosecution of war. The main axis of Viking aggression had shifted to the continent following their rebuff at Edington, so, with the exception of an attack on Kent which was rebuffed by the burgh of Colchester, for the first decade of its existence England faced only minor raids on its coastline.

Alfred pursued an active defence during this period politically and militarily. In 883 he scored a major political coup when Pope Marinus despatched a fragment of the True Cross to him, a vital tacit recognition by the universal Church of his claim to be King of the English. Ecclesiastical support represented a decisive weapon in Alfred's programme of nation building; potential rebels now risked their souls as heretics as well as their bodies as traitors. Furthermore, it also signalled papal acquiescence in Alfred's policy of taxing Church owned *bookland,* which would now become permanent in the interest of prosecuting the war against the heathen Viking. Building on this extended legitimacy, Alfred now claimed London, the most lucrative of all English burghs, seizing it in a surprise attack in 886. In addition to the wealth it brought, the stone walls of the city of London, its Roman bridge and the neighbouring burghs of Westminster and Southwark provided a quadruple defence of the River Thames, England's chief trading artery with the continent and an obvious invasion route into northern Wessex. From London, Alfred used his new navy to launch a series of amphibious assaults on Viking supply bases up the east coast, although the survival of the strongly fortified Viking port of Benfleet on the Essex side of the Thames estuary meant that the east coast remained vulnerable.

892-896: England's defences tested

Alfred's 'phoney war' ended in the 890s. The death of Guthrum in 890 was followed by the accession of the astute and bellicose Haestan, who made a show of continuing his predecessor's policy by agreeing to the baptism of his sons. Simultaneously, however, he planned a fresh offensive on Alfred's realm with Guthfrith, King of York. The defeat of the Vikings at the siege of Paris in 882 released substantial Viking forces under Harald Fairhair to support this offensive. Accordingly, a three pronged invasion of England was launched without warning in 892 – Guthfrith led a rapid advance along the western border of Mercia through Somerset and into Devon where he laid siege to Exeter, intending to split the western shires of England from its heartland. Haesten laid an amphibious force down the River Lea in East Anglia towards its linkup with the Thames, planning to storm London whilst Fairhair led a third army south west through Surrey towards Hampshire and the English capital of Winchester. This force was even larger and better coordinated than Guthrum's nearly decisive offensive against Wessex in 878.

The English defence in depth worked exactly as planned, sapping the momentum of each of Viking advances and giving Alfred's two field armies under the command of his son, Edward, and son-in-law, Aethelred, time to intercept them. As a result, Guthfrith was isolated from the rest of the Viking forces and compelled to retreat from Exeter by Aethelred, who eventually trapped him at Brignorth in Shropshire and compelled him to surrender. Heasten's force never left the River Lea, being stopped by a series of booms, whilst Fairhair was slowed by the burgh of Eashing in Surrey, enabling Edward to surprise and slaughter his army at the Battle of Farnham. Guthfrith and Haesten eventually agreed separate peace treaties along the model of Wedmore and withdrew into the Danelaw. The English victory was completed by the capture of Benfleet by Edward in 894.

The English victory is a testimony not only to Alfred's preparations but also to his successful development in command and control. Before 878 he and his predecessors tended to lead the field army of Wessex in person, risking the stability of the whole realm in the event of their deaths and leading to a failure to coordinate strategy across the kingdom. Moreover, despite his victory at Edington, Alfred was an indifferent general. Fortunately and wisely, he was realistic enough to accept it. Thus he played to his strengths by remaining at his capital of Winchester, serving as commander in chief of the English war effort, something at which he excelled. From Winchester he coordinated the actions of *burgh* garrisons, his navy, Athelred's Mercian field army and Edward's West Saxon field army. Together they systematically weakened and isolated the three Viking invasion forces. Taken together, the components of Alfred's war machine constitute perhaps the most efficient military in 9th century Europe, a war machine he and his successors successfully exploited to expand their territory and keep the Viking threat at bay for almost a century.

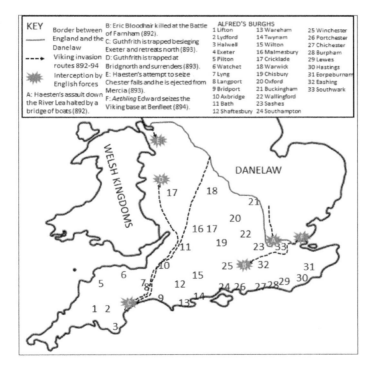

Fig. 11: Alfred's defence of England 878-899

893: Common Law

Alfred's issue of a new law code, or 'Doom Book', in 893 was the first sign of a national policy beyond the purely military. Its codicils are largely unremarkable and reflect contemporary practise in such matters, such as the establishment of rates of compensation, or *weregild,* for crimes and even accepted the role of private bloodfeuds as instruments of justice. In two respects, however, the code reveals a nation building agenda. The first can be seen in the apparently standard phrase that forms the first article of the code: "First, we enjoin, what is most necessary, that each man keep carefully his oath and pledge"[102]. Oath taking was at the heart of early medieval justice, but as Pollard observes[103], Alfred transformed its legal significance by requiring all free people over the age of 12 to swear an oath of loyalty to the king, unambiguously placing loyalty to him over any other bounds of obedience to family or personal lord. This universal oath of loyalty was a vital tool to Alfred and his successors as they sought to impose a standardised sense of loyalty and obedience over a disparate population. This was a population used to repeated betrayals and changes of side, particularly on the part of the *ealdormen*, most recently Wulfere of Wiltshire, whose betrayal almost cost Alfred his life in 878. Essentially, this universal oath of loyalty, the first of its kind in English history, made prosecution for treason definable, and thus also defined a link between loyalty to king and loyalty to kingdom.

Just as profound was the source of Alfred's law code which he clearly states in his Introduction:

'Then I, King Alfred, gathered them [previous laws] together and ordered to be written many of the ones that our forefathers observed... For I dared not presume to set down in writing at all many of my own, since it was unknown to me what would please them those who should come after us. But those which I found either in the days of Ine, my kinsmen, or of Offa, king of the Mercians, or of Aethelberht [king of Kent] (who first amongst the English people received

---

[102] Article 1 from 'Extracts from the Laws of King Alfred' in Keynes S. and Lapidge M. (2004) p. 164
[103] Pollard (2005) pp. 256-7

baptism), and which seemed to me to be most just, I collected herein, and omitted the others.'[104]

Had Alfred simply imposed a law code based on the laws of Wessex laid down by his predecessor, Ine, on his realm he could have been viewed as an imperialist conqueror, as Offa had in the 8th century, or his own grandfather Egbert in the 9th. That his universal code combined elements of the legal codes of the most celebrated rulers of Wessex, Mercia and Kent; Ine, Offa and Aethelberht respectively was a public relations stroke of genius. The disparate peoples of Alfred's new kingdom of England, Cornish, West Saxons, South Saxons, Kentishmen and Mercians alike were presented with a new code of law genuinely national in its origin and vision. It is in fact the foundation of Common Law, a legal system based on precedent of such robustness that it not only survived as a basis for law throughout the Anglo-Saxon period, but was retained by Norman and Plantagenet kings post-Conquest and makes repeated appearances in the charters of kings seeking to uphold the legitimacy of their rule, most famously King John's Magna Carta. At one unconfrontational stroke, Alfred's law code laid down the first precedent for a united England. And where law led, culture would follow.

896-99: *Kulturkampf*

Had Alfred confined his activities to military victory he would be remembered today as a distinguished general, but not as 'the Great'. What earns him his unique place in English history is his singular vision of an English nation state and the resourceful means by which he transformed vision into reality. Administratively and economically, by 896 Alfred had already gone a considerable way towards welding his disparate realm into one nation – the extension of the shire and burgh system created an extremely efficient common system of local government and defence, whilst his coinage reordering in the 880s provides a successful early example of the use of the institution of a common currency for the combined purposes of

---

[104] Introduction 49.9 from 'Extracts from the Laws of King Alfred' in Keynes S. and Lapidge M. (2004) p. 164

promoting trade, simplifying tax and promoting integration along the lines of the euro. Nonetheless, 'England' in 896 was less a nation state, more a massive armed camp whose inhabitants were bound together primarily by the threat of a common enemy rather than a common identity.

The last phase of Alfred's life was devoted to achieving this common identity through the active promotion of England as a nation state – the pioneer of a process which would be defined in the 19th century as *kulturkampf* – 'cultural struggle'. Part of this, the first national education programme, was the product of Alfred's particular brand of piety. For Alfred, scholarliness was quite literally next to godliness. It was his sincerely held belief that the decay in English learning, which had occurred in the century before his life, was one of the reasons why God withdrew His favour from the English people and allowed the Viking blight to descend upon them. Crucially however, his education programme did not involve a restoration of the Latin based learning of his forebears. In a startlingly egalitarian move, his educational renaissance was based around the vernacular – the Old English spoken by contemporary society. Hence he arranged for certain key texts which he deemed 'most necessary for all men to know' to be translated into Old English. Uniquely, many of these were undertaken personally by Alfred, making him the only royal author of the early medieval England. The prefaces he wrote to these translations provide a window into his thinking:

'Therefore it seems better to me, if it seems so to you, that we also translate certain books, which are most needful for all men to know, into that language that we all can understand, and accomplish this, as with God's help we may very easily do if we have peace, so that all the youth of free men now in England who have the means to apply themselves to it, be set to learning, while they are not useful for any other occupation, until they know how to read English writing well'.[105]

Parallel to these translations was the beginning of a programme of

---

[105] Alfred's prose preface to Gregory the Great's *Pastoral Care*. In Ed. Keynes S. and Lapidge M. (London, 2004).

school creation across England, usually centred on cathedrals and minsters. Teachers were drawn from the clergy, pupils from the ranks of the English middle classes as well as the nobility. Alfred lived long enough to see the establishment of a school for his courtiers based on Winchester Old Minster which served as a model for other institutions. The majority of these institutions were, however, the work of his son, Edward, and grandson, Athelstan, who continued his programme. The very concept of a national education system therefore had its origins in Alfred's vision. Indeed a handful of schools from this first tranche survive to the present day, such as Somerset's Wells Cathedral School, founded in 909 by Edward.

Alfred's apparently altruistic educational policy nonetheless had a political undertone. A literate population was not only more godly, but also provided the king with an efficient governing class. Moreover, Alfred's books 'most necessary for all men to know' were chosen by the king specifically because they projected his world view – his translations of Gregory the Great's *Pastoral Care*, Boethius' *Consolation of Philosophy*, St Augustine's *Soliloquies* and the first fifty psalms of the Psalter combine piety, with a call for self-discipline and obedience to hierarchy. Furthermore, as Alfred himself concedes, his translations were not solely driven by a desire to reproduce the original text as accurately as possible; he does tweak the original meanings to make them both more accessible and more closely conforming to his own views: 'I translated not word for word but sense for sense'.[106]

The Alfred Jewel – greatest surviving treasure of Alfred's *kulturkampf*. Discovered near Atheleney in 1693 it is believed to have been the ornamental cap of an *aestel*, a gilded stick used to assist reading. It is inscribed 'Alfred commanded me to be made'.

---

[106] Ibid.

143

Alfred's educational programme was integral to a much wider vision of a united nation state under a Cerdicynn ruler. In the pursuit of this he carefully cultivated a public image in a manner that reveals the more calculating side of his personality. Any nation needs a national story, and to this end Alfred had *Bede's Ecclesiastical History* translated into Old English as part of his renaissance in learning. But he supplemented it by two works which consciously embedded himself and his family into national epic – the *Anglo-Saxon Chronicle* and Asser's *Life of Alfred,* both of which represent the recent wars against the Vikings as struggles of national awakening in which Alfred's position as rightful ruler of the whole of the English race by blood, by popular acclamation and by divine will is repeatedly asserted:

"The same year also King Alfred fortified the city of London; and the whole English nation turned to him, except that part of it which was held captive by the Danes."[107]

'He alone, sustained by the divine aid, like a skilful pilot, strove to steer his ship, laden with much wealth, into the safe and much desired harbour of his country, though almost all his crew were tired, and suffered them not to faint or hesitate, though sailing amid the manifold waves and eddies of this present life.'[108]

Through these works, Alfred presents himself as fulfilling God's divine plan for the unification of England and as the worthy inheritor of the crown of former English kings. Significantly, despite its Christian author and subject, Asser's biography begins by a genealogy of Alfred which traces his legitimacy through the first king of Wessex, Cerdic, back to legendary descent from the Anglo-Saxon father god, Woden. Significantly too, Asser consciously apes the style of saints' hagiographies in his account, portraying Alfred not as a two dimensional ideal, but as a fallible human who, by God's grace, attains sufficient wisdom to overcome his tribulations and in so doing becomes a role model. By taking on the behaviour of a living saint, Alfred was identifying

---

[107] *Anglo-Saxon Chronicle* entry for the year 886 E.H.D. Vol. 1.
[108] Asser's *Life of King Alfred* paragraph 109 in Ed. Keynes S. and Lapidge M. (London, 2004)

himself with a vibrant tradition of English sainthood, including Oswald, Bede and Cuthbert and in so doing added another tier to his carefully contrived legitimacy. Under Alfred and his successors therefore, as art historian Janina Ramirez has noted, 'There started to be a sense that sanctity could be harnessed to the political needs of 'the nation'.[109]

Alfred's final legacy was a secure succession based on a realistic appraisal of the political reality of England at the end of the 9th century. Despite his determined *kulturkampf*, Alfred accepted that the complete subjugation of former loyalties into a united English identity could not be completed during his lifetime, particularly in Mercia. Accordingly, he was careful to preserve the notion of Mercian self-government in life and in death – and thus his will divided his realm, the Mercian portion going to Aethelred, *ealdorman* of Mercia and his wife, Alfred's daughter, Aethelflead, and the rest to his eldest son, Edward. To prepare this triumvirate for rule, in the last years of his life Alfred retreated into a supervisory form of kingship, allowing his son, daughter and son-in-law to exercise the bulk of governance. As a result, when Alfred died prematurely in 899, possibly of Crohn's disease, a realm which had seemed on the verge of collapse just 21 years earlier was united, secure and emerging as the world's first nation state.

The clearest contemporary verdict on Alfred's legacy comes from the king himself: "My will was to live worthily as long as I lived, and after my life to leave to them that should come after, my memory in good works"[110]. Behind these words of pious humility, Alfred emerges as a genuinely remarkable ruler, a juxtaposition of ruthless warlord, relentless self-publicist and visionary nation builder. His career provides one of history's most unambiguous examples of an individual who transformed the world in which he lived. It is not an exaggeration to state that without him a united England would never have come into being.

---

[109]Cited in Elton M. 'Interview with Dr Janina Ramirez' in *BBC History Magazine* August 2015.
[110] Alfred's prose preface to Boethius' *Consolation of Philosophy*. in Ed. Keynes S. and Lapidge M. (London, 2004)

Historiography

Medieval:

The Anglo Saxon Chronicle

Asser's Life of Alfred

Prefaces to Alfred's translations

Current debate:

Richard Abels in *Alfred the Great: War, Kingship and Culture in Anglo-Saxon England* (London, 1998) argues that the unique place accorded to Alfred is justified. He opines that Alfred's unique combination of successful warrior, political pragmatist and determined intellectual merits the epithet 'the Great'. We should be wary of idealising Alfred, however, Abels feels, for the king was very much a man of his time, for example executing prisoners without a moment's hesitation in a manner that modern society would find repellent. Indeed, Abels believes that it is as the perfect early medieval king that we should view Alfred.

David Horspool's *Alfred the Great* (Stroud, 2004) argues that Alfred's contribution was pivotal in ensuring the survival of an independent English state and culture, but that his unique reputation in early modern English history is primarily due to the greater volume of written evidence that survives from his reign. A realistic view of his contribution should place him the context of a steadily developing notion of English nation statehood that began with Offa and was essentially completed by Alfred's son Edward.

Justin Pollard in *Alfred the Great: The man who made England* (London, 2005) agrees with Starkey's view that Alfred was the visionary creator of England, the world's first nation state, but argues that the king's rise to this unique position was less meteoric, more the result of learning from early failure. In particular, he highlights how Alfred's royally sanctioned texts have glossed over the collapse in confidence in his rule that accompanied the events of 878 leading to open conspiracy between the Vikings and disaffected elements within the king's own court.

David Pratt in *The Political Thought of King Alfred the Great* (Cambridge University Press, 2007) plays down the uniqueness of Alfred's ideas, arguing instead that they represent a particularly successful combination of contemporary trends in government, society and faith. To the end of his reign, Pratt argues, Alfred remained in his heart king of Wessex not of England, transforming it into an efficient militarised state on the lines of Sparta via a 'coordinated reordering of his assembled kingdom'[111], but that the ingenious use of royal sanctioned texts did such an effective job of presenting Alfred as the perfect king ('ubiquitous lord'[112]) that Englishmen outside Wessex were happy to subordinate themselves to his rule and that of his successors.

David Starkey in *The Monarchy of England* (London, 2004) takes a maximalist view of Alfred's contribution, believing him to be the fount out of which the English nation sprang fully formed. In particular, he argues that it was through Alfred's unique vision that England emerged as the first nation state, placing particular emphasis on the political dimension of his cultural programme, hence his use of the aggressively nationalistic German term *kulturkampf* to describe the process.

Barbara Yorke in 'Alfred the Great: The most perfect man in history?' (*History Today* Volume 49 Issue 10 November 1999) argues that Alfred's exceptional reputation owes more to his utility as the embodiment of English values to later generations of Englishmen. The fact that he was never canonised by the papacy meant that he was an acceptable role model to post-Reformation Tudors, Stuarts and Hanoverians, whilst to the Victorians he became a symbol of English racial supremacy. Whilst she concedes that his contribution to English history was profound, she argues that Alfred and Asser's carefully

---

[111] Pratt D. *he Political Thought of King Alfred the Great* (Cambridge University Press, 2007) pp. 349-50
[112] Ibid. p. 338

constructed propaganda obscured his true value when compared to his peers.

Questions to consider
- To what extent is Alfred's ultimate success against the Vikings explained by his character?

- Assess the view that the main achievement of King Alfred was defending Wessex against the Viking Danes.

- 'Alfred's reputation depends as much on cultural achievements as on military successes.' Assess the validity of this claim.

- How well does Alfred deserve his historical reputation as 'the Great'?

Chapter 9: Wessex victorious – the Golden Age of the Anglo-Saxon monarchy

Cerdicynn dynasty kings during the 'Hegemony of Wessex'

Alfred 'the Great' 871-899: Decisively defeats the Vikings, First King of 'all the English'.

Edward 'the Elder' 899-924: Conquers all English land up to the Humber

Aethelflaed 'Lady of the Mercians' 911-918: De facto queen of Mercia

Athelstan 'the Glorious' 924-933: Conqueror of Northumbria, first king of a united England

Edmund 'the Magnificent' 933-946: European diplomat

Eadred 952-55: Subjugator of the Northumbrian rebellion

Eadwig 955-959: Enemy of the Church

Edgar 'the Peaceable' 959-975: Currency reformer and devisor of 'imperial' coronation

Key events

903: Aethelwold rebellion fails

910: Edward the Elder secures Mercia after the battle of Tettenhall

918: Death of Athelflaed sees Mercia fully subsumed within England

937: Battle of Brunaburgh seals Athelstan's conquest of Northumbria – united England from this point onwards

954: Defeat of Northumbrian Viking king Eric Bloodaxe

970s: Edgar establishes national mints

973: Imperial coronation of Edgar at Bath marks high point of the majesty of the Cerdicynn dynasty

Edward, Aethelflaed and the conquest of the midlands

The proto-realm of England may have been relatively secure from external threats on the death of Alfred in 899, but internal strife remained. As has already been observed, the rule of primogeniture did not apply in Wessex, and Alfred had instituted a new convention of succession, whereby the next king was to be appointed by his predecessor with the assent of the *witan*. Being both astute and a proven war leader, Edward the Elder, Alfred's eldest son, had received such approval before his father's death. Unfortunately at the exact moment when unity was paramount, an alternative *atheling* appeared – Edward's cousin, Athelwold. The *Anglo-Saxon Chronicle*, unusually detailed in its description of these events, relates how Aethelwald went as far as securing backing for his claim from the Viking kingdoms who used this breech in the Cerdicynn family to launch a fresh invasion of Wessex. This ended with the scrappy, unintentional Battle of the Holme in 902, in which, fortuitously, both Athelwold and the Viking commander Eohric were killed, automatically bringing the rebellion to a close. Nonetheless, it is an indication of how formidable the Viking army remained that Edward sustained losses large enough to oblige an immediate truce: King Edward, from necessity, concluded a peace both with the army of East Anglia and of Northumbria'[113].

It is likely that Edward would have desired a continuation of his father's plan of nation building and territorial expansion in any case, but the near-run defeat of Aethelwold's rebellion made it a certainty, as it indicated how precarious England's position remained in relation to the Viking threat. 'England' at this stage essentially consisted of Wessex and its dependent territories of Cornwall, Sussex and Kent, plus the rump of Mercia, the latter ground down by Viking invasion, but still proud and independent-minded, with neither people nor nobility ready to be subsumed within Alfred's 'England'. The nominally independent rule of the native Earldoman, Aethelred, as 'Lord of Mercia' had ameliorated Mercian sensibilities during Alfred's reign and the

---

[113] *Anglo Saxon Chronicle* entry for the year 906. E.H.D. Vol. I

first half of Edward's. Aethelred was wholly dependent on Wessex support for his throne and, as a sign of this, had married Alfred's eldest daughter, Aethelflaed. He was less of a puppet, more of an able and proactive lieutenant of the Cerdicynns and thus his death in 911 created something of a crisis in Wessex-Mercian relations. The remarkable Aethelflaed (depicted below), who may well have played a part in the government of Mercia anyway towards the end of Aethelred's life, presented the perfect solution – a capable, experienced ruler who enjoyed the confidence of the Mercians and who by blood was firmly within the sphere of influence of Wessex. It is indicative of how compelling a case she made that both the ruling councils of Mercia and Wessex overcame the deep seated cultural objection to female rule and named her as ruler or 'Lady' of Mercia, a position she would hold for over seven years.

Edward the Elder and Aethelflead, Lady of the Mercians from a 14th century geneology - the unique brother and sister team who reconquered Mercia and East Anglia in the early 10th century, building on their father Alfred's dream of a united England.

The fact that both these councils, plus Edward the Elder, were so uncharacteristically accepting of female rule may also indicate that Aethelflaed was already fulfilling one the key roles of an Anglo-Saxon monarch prior to Aethelred's death by acting as war leader. In total defiance of contemporary notions of gender, Aethelflead seems to have played an active role in commanding the Mercian army from the English victory at Tettenhall onwards; in fact she may have led troops in battle personally, as the *Anglo-Saxon Chronicle* relates of her actions against the Vikings in the year 917:

'This year Aethelflead, lady of the Mercians, with the help of God... conquered the town called Derby, with all that thereto belonged; and there were also slain four of her *thegns*, that were most dear to her, within the gates'.[114]

Above all, it is evidence of pragmatism on Edward's part. Clearly he had no desire to share rule with his sister; his choice of the ancient Mercian stone of kings at Kingston-upon-Thames for his coronation in 900 is indicative of his ambitions towards Mercia. However he did not let resentment or animosity cloud his relations with Aethelflead; for the remainder of her life the two siblings worked together in a unique and highly successful relationship that saw the Vikings driven out of Mercia, Essex and East Anglia.

Edward and Aethelflead's advance had none of the caution and repeated pauses for treaties of their father. From the outset it was aggressive, systematic and followed a pattern that maximised English strengths of numbers and expertise in fortress building to neutralise the Viking advantage in combat experience and mobility. It began with the purchasing of land by English nobles on the Viking side of the border on the instructions of the royal family to create footholds from which attacks could be supplied. Each advance would begin with surprise raids into Viking territory designed to weaken resistance. Following this, flying columns of English troops would advance to a strategically significant position behind enemy lines, either capture the fortress, if one existed, or hastily build a turf walled *burgh*. Edward commanded the army of Wessex in the east which worked in close cooperation with Aethelflaed and the Mercian army in the west, carefully timing their movement so that Viking opposition was caught between two advances and unable to deal decisively with either. These burghs, such as Chester and Runcorn in the west, and Derby and Bakewell in the east, posed an intolerable threat to the Viking frontier defences, requiring the Vikings to

---

[114] *Ibid.* entry for the year 917

mount costly and invariably unsuccessful sieges.

This policy of the offensive use of burghs was extremely innovative, anticipating the Norman use of motte and bailey castles in the 11th century. Its systematic application from 909 to 917 haemorrhaged Viking manpower and, by pushing their forces ever further north and east, made it progressively harder for the Viking rulers of Northumbria, Mercia and East Anglia to coordinate their operations. In 917, whilst the Northumbrian and Mercian Vikings were occupied by Aethelflaed's siege of Derby, Edward decisively took the initiative, abandoning his policy of advance and consolation in favour of a rapid strike on the East Anglian Viking headquarters of Tempsford. Edward's forces killed the Viking king and his principle lieutenants. As a result of this decapitation, remaining Viking forces in East Anglia and Essex immediately surrendered to Edward at Colchester, wherein, 'Many people who had been under the rule of the Danes for nearly 30 years both in East Anglia and Essex submitted to him, that they would agree to all he would, and would keep peace with whomever the king wished to keep peace, both at land and sea'.[115]

Politically, as well as militarily, the victory of Tempsford represents a seismic change in the balance of power between English and Vikings. Before its full implications could be realised, however, Athelflaed died at Tamworth in 918, bequeathing Mercia to her daughter, Aelfwyn, with the support of the council of Mercia. Remarkably this was the only time in English history succession passed from a mother to her daughter. This time Edward did not compromise, however, using his victorious army to seize Mercia, exile Aelfwyn to a nunnery and proclaim himself king of Mercia. The level of opposition he encountered is unclear; the *Anglo-Saxon Chronicle* simply recording that 'All the nation in the land of the Mercians which had been subject to Aethelflaed submitted to him';[116]. What is clear is that it was effective; within six months Edward felt confident enough to march on Nottingham, one of the last Mercian towns in Viking hands, and seize it.

---

[115] Ibid, entry for the year 917
[116] Ibid, entry for the year 918

Nottingham, with its large Danish population, added a new element to the increasingly ethnically diverse realm of England. Danes, East Angles, East Saxons and Mercians alike now found themselves subject to the unfamiliar rule of the Cerdicynns. That this potentially explosive cocktail did not erupt in rebellion in Edward's lifetime is testament not only to his formidable reputation as a war leader, but also his sensitive application of his father's policy of toleration. In the new realms he had conquered, Edward encountered many English who had been dispossessed and persecuted by the Vikings, and some sort of ethnic backlash seemed inevitable. Yet somehow Edward avoided it, as Humble notes, 'The Reconquest did not end in the extermination or even expulsion of the beaten Danes, but in a most liberal amnesty and forward looking spirit'.[117] Instead, as the *Anglo-Saxon Chronicle* makes clear, the new Danish subjects of Edward were to be accorded the same rights and responsibilities as his new English subjects. After the capture of Nottingham, for instance, Edward ordered the town walls 'to be repaired and manned both with English and Danes. And all the people who had settled in Mercia, both Danish and English, submitted to him'[118].

In one respect Edward was the beneficiary of circumstance. His enlightened policy of toleration coincided with a fresh transfusion of predatory Vikings from Ireland arriving in Northumbria whose raids posed a threat to Dane and Englishman alike. Secure in their lands, we now find the remarkable spectacle of the settled ex-Vikings of Mercia and East Anglia making common cause with the English in defence of their property against immigrant Vikings. Such a division of the Danish population of England between settlers and raiders was essential for the cohesion of the new realm as it meant that future Viking invasions would not benefit from a 'fifth column' of support within English lands.

919-20 saw the completion of the reconquest of Mercia. By 917 Edward's eastern advance had reached the River Humber, the natural border

---

[117] Humble, R (1980) p.78
[118] *Anglo-Saxon Chronicle*, entry for the year 918

between Mercia and Northumbria. The westward drive to reach its equivalent, the Mersey, had been halted by Aethelflaed's death, leaving a vulnerable no-man's land in what would become north Cheshire and Derbyshire. The creation of frontier burghs at Runcorn and Derby eliminated this weakness, and indeed Edward felt strong enough to cross over into Northumbrian territory for the first time in the north west, crossing the Mersey to establish a final burgh on the site of the old Roman fort of Manchester. This would serve as both early warning of Viking invasion and a jumping off point for an advance into Northumbria.

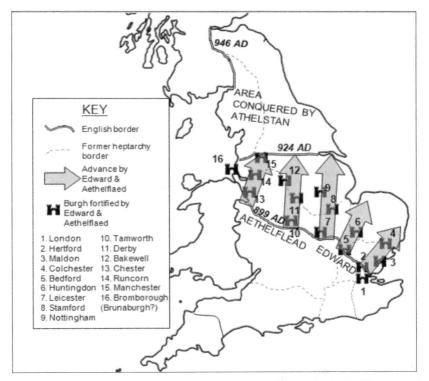

Fig 12: The unification of England under Edward, Aethelflaed and Athelstan 899-946.

Edward never attempted the conquest of Northumbria. Perhaps worn out by his efforts, he spent his last four years in comparative peace before dying in 924. Unsurprisingly, given the almost continual campaigns of conquest during his reign, his record was chiefly that of a warrior rather than a politician or social reformer in the mould of his father. That said, he must surely have undertaken some administrative reform to consolidate his conquests – Stenton believes that the extension of the Wessex shire system throughout western Mercia took place in the last years of his reign[119], a system which cut across the tribal and administrative divisions of Mercia, perhaps in a deliberate attempt to erode local loyalties. The eastern half of Mercia, East Anglia and Essex, which had been reorganised and extensively settled by the Danes, were reformed more cautiously. The latter, of course, survives today as a shire in its own right, whilst most of eastern Mercia was lumped together into a 'super shire', Lincolnshire, which roughly conformed to the land formerly held by the Danish army of Stamford.

The only other area of reform under Edward that we are aware of is episcopal. The land that Edward conquered was still largely Christian in belief, but the structure of the Church had been shattered by Viking depredations – its cathedrals, in particular, lay in ruins. Indeed some, such as Lindsay, were never re-established. Remarkably, however, Edward's reforms targeted not these institutions, but those of the comparatively unscathed heartland of Wessex: The previously excessively large dioceses of Winchester and Sherborne were broken down into five new ones and in the case of Wells, and possibly others, a cathedral school was instituted, suggesting Edward was following a continuation of his father's education campaign.

Edward's legacy to his son and heir, Athelstan, was rather a mixed one therefore. Militarily he was undeniably successful; under his campaigns and those of his sister the initiative had turned decisively in the Cerdicynns favour and England had gone from being an embattled and fragile hypothetical state into an aggressive conqueror feared by its neighbours. That said, it seems Edward lacked either the time or the inclination to systemically restore the damage done to the areas conquered by the Danes. Moreover, in the year of

---

[119] Stenton (1971) pp.336-37. The author does concede however that this is a hypothesis, the first specific mention of a Mercian shire, Cheshire, does not occur until 980.

his death, he finally faced a serious rebellion from the Mercians, in the vulnerable north western corner where the men of Chester apparently challenged his rule with the aid of the Welsh princes. It was whilst dealing with this revolt that the now aged Edward died. Edward had more than doubled the size of his father's realm, but it was neither as stable nor as prosperous as it needed to be if short term conquest was to be turned into long term assimilation. Furthermore, although the *Anglo-Saxon Chronicle* states that remaining independent Celtic and Viking rulers within Britain 'chose him to be their father and lord,'[120] this seems to have been a nominal and short term submission of overlordship made to Edward alone. Sihtric, Viking king of Northumbria, in particular, seems to have renounced any obedience to the Cerdicynns on Edward's death.

Athelstan, first king of England

A 10th century illustration of Athelstan shown presenting a book to St Cuthbert.

---

[120] *Anglo-Saxon Chronicle* entry for the year 920 in E.H.D. Vol. 1

Edward's son, Athelstan, would prove an extraordinarily astute ruler. Having spent much of his youth in Aethelflaed's Mercian court at Tamworth, he was far better placed to gain the loyalty of the Mercians than his father. However, allegations of illegitimacy meant that before he could be crowned he had to defeat a sizable faction opposed to his rule in Wessex favouring his brother, Aelfweard. William of Malmesbury euphemistically hints at the struggle Athelstan must have undertaken to ensure his legitimacy was recognised by all the *ealdormen* of his kingdom: 'He trampled down and destroyed envy by the glory of his virtues, and after the death of his father and the decease of his brother he was crowned king at Kingston'[121]. The 'decease of his brother' refers to Aelfweard's extremely convenient death, just 16 days after his father's, a fortuitous coincidence. Or, perhaps more likely, an early demonstration of the ruthless streak that Athelstan would employ to tremendous effect during his life.

Apart from Aelfweard, the chronicler Simeon of Durham also records the grisly treatment Athelstan meted out to his brother Edwin, 'King Athelstan ordered his brother Edwin to be drowned at sea'[122]. Athelstan's relations with his numerous other brothers appear to have been harmonious, indeed Edmund, who would ultimately succeed the childless Athelstan, seems to have effectively operated as his lieutenant in governance and war. An early sign of the strength of the new king's position was a diplomatic mission from Sihtric proposing a formal dynastic alliance in 926, the outcome of which was the marriage of the Northumbrian king to an unnamed sister of Athelstan. This brought the promise of peace to northern England as Sihtric had managed to unite the predatory Irish Vikings under his rule as well as those of Northumbria. Within months, however, Sihtric died and a dangerous power vacuum emerged, with two competing heirs Olaf and Guthfrith. Civil war resulted, both claimants seeking the intervention of the other major powers in the north – the Kings of Scotland and Strathclyde and the independent English lord of Bamborough.

---

[121] William of Malmesbury *Gestis Regum Anglorum* Chapter 8 paragraph 133
[122] Simeon of Durham *History of the kings* Chapter 6 Ibid.

Athelstan decided against backing either claimant. Rather he took advantage of the situation to complete the conquest of the English lands. In 927 Athelstan compelled Strathclyde, Scotland and Bamborough to make a separate treaty with him at Eamont, near Penrith, acknowledging his claim to the Northumbrian throne, a political manoeuvre that left the Vikings isolated. He followed this up by speedily occupying the Viking capital York and demolishing its walls, compelling the surrender of the disunited Vikings.

The conquest of English lands completed, Athelstan's policy turned to consolidation. Between 927 and 931 he secured overlordship of the Welsh princes, at Hereford, as well as the Cornish, whose border he formalised at the River Tamar. He also organised a punitive raiding expedition into Scotland in reaction to an unknown slight, for the first time in English history undertaking a joint operation between his navy and army, a sign of the growing sophistication of what, by now, must have been extremely battle hardened armed forces.

As Edward the Elder found, however, conquest did not equal acceptance. Many of Athelstan's new Northumbrian subjects did not accept his rule, whilst to the Scots, Strathclyders, Welsh, Irish and above all Vikings he was a threat to their independent existence. Inevitably a coalition formed against him, the death of Guthfrith in 934 meaning that Olaf Sihtricsson was able to reunify the Vikings of Ireland and Northumbria. Under his leadership a huge joint expedition; which also included Scots and Strathclyders; swept Athelstan's navy aside and landed in Northumbria. From there they sought to invade England. Athelstan and his brother, Edmund, mobilised the armies of Wessex and Mercia to meet them. The location of the ensuing Battle of Brunaburgh remains unconfirmed to us,[123] but given it featured the largest armies that the two sides were capable of putting together, the result was inevitably decisive.

---

[123] Wood favours a location near Rotherham in Yorkshire, however a team at the University of Nottingham led by Professor Steve Harding has provided recent and more compelling evidence for the Wirral, the peninsula between the Dee and Mersey estuaries based on the modern place names 'Bromborough' (Bruna's fort?) and the nearby Dingmere ('Ding' or 'Thing' being the Norse word for a parliament or council) in *The Independent* 8.12.04.

Unusually, the events of the battle are recorded in detail, in the form of an epic poem *The Battle of Brunaburgh* preserved in its entirety in the *Anglo-Saxon Chronicle* which presents a vivid picture of the devastating effects of 10th century battle:

'Edward's sons clove the shield-wall, hewed the linden-wood shields with hammered swords, for it was natural for men of their lineage to defend their land, their treasure and their homes, in frequent battle against every foe. Their enemies perished; the Scots and the pirates fell doomed. The field grew dark with the blood of men... There lay many a man destroyed by the spears, many a northern warrior shot over shield; and likewise many a Scot lay weary, sated with battle'.[124]

Despite its protestations that this was a defensive battle against invaders, the poem continues with an unapologetic account of the relentless pursuit of the fleeing allies by Athelstan and Edmund who reportedly took no prisoners and killed eleven Vikings princes as well as the son of Constantine II, king of Scotland. Laconically, it concludes:

'Never yet in this island... was a greater slaughter of a host made by the edge of a sword, since the Angles and Saxons came hither from the east'.[125]

Setting aside inevitable poetic license, Brunaburgh completed the process of counterattack begun at Edington seventy years earlier. Politically, its obvious short term consequence was the elimination of any remaining threat to unification of England: Olaf Sihtricsson returned to Ireland with the wreck of an army, incapable of further offensive action; Constantine II of Scotland was an old and disillusioned man who shortly retired to a monastery. From this point on, although there would be renewed rebellion on and off for another century, the Northumbrian Danes and English appear to have cut their losses and embraced the rule of the Cerdicynns. For this reason the historical convention is to date the formal unification of England to 937 – the

---

[124] 'The Battle of Brunaburgh' in *The Anglo-Saxon Chronicle*, entry for the year 937 in E.H.D. Vol. 1
[125] Ibid.

year of Brunaburgh.

When not at war, Athelstan appears to have devoted much of his reign to resolving the tangle of land disputes that inevitably arose across a realm so recently conquered and reconquered. The comparatively large volume of state papers surviving from his reign is a testimony to the systematic way he dealt with these challenges. His desire for consensus from as broad a sector of the population as possible indicates that he clearly understood that a fair settlement of land ownership was essential for the completion of the process of state building he had inherited from his father and grandfather. His charter granting the estate of Amounderness to the Archdiocese of York, for example, combines dire threats to anyone who defies the treaty with national consensus in the form of countersignatures by 18 bishops, 27 English nobles, two Welsh kings and seven Danish nobles.[126]

Athelstan was able to achieve such consensus through his innovative development of the Wessex institution of the Witan. The king seems to have periodically summoned a Witan of all England, comprising the secular and clerical leadership of the entire kingdom and its neighbours, both English and non-English and led them in a form of Parliament to resolve both land disputes and seek counsel on matters of national policy. He rotated these Witans of all England between the north and south of the country, using the Archbishops of York and Canterbury respectively to second his authority. The spectacle of unparalleled royal power allied with the universal authority of the Church seems to have ensured there was little resistance to Athelstan's will.

Greater control over his realm gave Athelstan more time to pursue a coherent foreign policy. From the reign of Offa onwards, there is considerable evidence of correspondence and treaties between English and continental rulers, indeed Alfred married one of his daughters, Aelfthryth, to the Count of Flanders. However, Athelstan's foreign relations were both more consistent and more successful than any other Anglo-Saxon king. He maintained

---

[126] Grant by King Athelstan of Amounderness to the church of York (7 June 934) Ibid. Charter no. 104 pp.550-551.

11th century illustration of the king and his Witan – the attending ealdormen wear conical hats of office.

excellent relations with the papacy, essential not only for maintaining his ability to levy tax on church owned 'bookland', but also at the start of his reign necessary to shore up the precarious legitimacy of his claim to the throne – William of Malmesbury records how 'a certain Alfred' who accused Athelstan of illegitimacy was despatched to Rome to make an oath before the Pope and promptly dropped dead after committing perjury[127].

Moreover, Athelstan excelled at using matrimony to further his own legitimacy and that of his dynasty, being blessed by four sisters. One of these, as we have already noted, was married to Sihtric of Northumbria in the period immediately before Athelstan's invasion. A more lasting result was obtained by the marriage of Eadhild to Hugh, Duke of the Franks, and Edith to Henry the Fowler, Holy Roman Emperor. This double dynastic alliance between the Cerdicynns and the two leading rulers in Europe represents a unique achievement on Athelstan's part, unmatched by any English king until the Reformation, and confirmed that England, under Athelstan, had joined France, the Holy Roman and Byzantine Empires as the foremost powers in 10th century Europe.

---

[127] William of Malmesbury Ibid. p.303

These alliances also brought highly desirable gifts from Athelstan's new brothers-in-law: The sword of Constantine the Great, the first Roman Emperor to convert to Christianity with one of the nails of the cross set in its hilt; the lance that had pieced Christ's side at the crucifixion and fragments of both the cross and the crown of thorns. Whatever the authenticity of these pieces, possession of them by Athelstan added yet more prestige and sanctity to his reign, the English brand of Catholicism being particularly noted for its devotion to relics. Relic collecting seems to have been more than a political tool for Athelstan, it was a hobby that towards the end of his life verged on obsession. This reflects the deep personal piety of a king who seems to have consciously embraced a life of celibacy, made possible because his three younger brothers and their numerous offspring provided all the heirs the dynasty needed. Happily for England, Athelstan's piety was a marketable asset, as Humble writes, 'The English king's piety lubricated diplomatic exchanges, encouraged the advancement of art and culture in England and stimulated the pilgrim traffic... with resultant financial benefits to the host country'.[128]

Athelstan only reigned for nine years. However, such was his energy and particularly effective blend of personal piety, military acumen and political shrewdness, that within this time he not only achieved his grandfather's dream of English unity through conquest, but he was able to substantially advance that conquest along the road to nation statehood. The reality of England that Edmund inherited in 933 was as much Athelstan's achievement as Alfred's.

Edmund the consolidator

Only 18 years old when he assumed the throne in 939, Edmund was already a respected warrior by virtue of the part he had played at Brunaburgh. He would need this prowess from the outset, for his reign was dominated by northern rebellion. Taking advantage of the distraction caused by Edmund's

---

[128] Humble (1980) p.83

coronation ceremony at Kingston, Irish Viking Olaf Guthfrithson staged a successful coup in what we must now call northern England, seizing York and proclaiming himself King of Northumbria. Many of Athelstan's newly erected burghs withstood the Viking assault, but were left isolated. Organised resistance was stifled by the unexpected defection of the Archbishop of York, Wulfstan, who broke the traditional consensus of ecclesiastical support for the Cerdicynns' nation building by openly calling for a partition of England into north and south. He was undoubtedly influenced by resentment at the subordination of the Archdiocese of York to Canterbury, an issue known as the primacy dispute which was to fester into the 14th century, but there is no doubt this call for partition mirrored ongoing resentment on the part of many northern lords, both English and Danish, as to what they saw as the imposition of alien rule from the south.

Olaf Guthfrithson was clearly a formidable warrior and a good politician, for he was able to persuade a sizeable part of Northumbria and northern Mercia to defect to his rule, going as far as seizing Tamworth, the Mercian capital in 940. This induced the Danish overlord of the old Danelaw 'Five Boroughs' of Leicester, Nottingham, Derby, Stamford and Lincoln to defect and Edmund was obliged to concede a treaty negotiated by the Archbishops of York and Canterbury which essentially renounced rule over much of the land his predecessors, Edward and Athelstan, had conquered in the previous decades. It was the greatest defeat sustained by the Cerdicynns since Alfred's flight to Athelney in 878.

Mortality saved Edmund. in 942 Olaf Guthrfithson died, apparently of natural causes, leaving his new realm to his timid cousin Olaf Sihtricsson. Edmund immediately reconquered the Five Boroughs, Tamworth and the rest of northern Mercia. The *Anglo-Saxon Chronicle*, unsurprisingly very brief in its description of the embarrassing period of 940-42, suddenly returns to detail in describing these events, explaining how Edmund, like Athelstan, was able to exploit the division between the settled Danes of Mercia and their raiding contemporaries from Northumbria: 'The Danes were previously subjected by force under the Norsemen, for a long time in bonds of captivity to the heathens, until the defender of warriors, the son of Edward, King Edmund, redeemed them, to his glory'.[129]

His siege of Leicester in 943 resulted in the secret escape of both Olaf Sihtricsson and Archbishop Wulfstan and was the final straw for the Northumbrian Vikings. They deposed Olaf and replaced him with Raegnald Guthfrithson. A power vacuum ensued, with both Viking rulers actively courting Edmund for recognition of their position, even going as far as to submit to baptism with him as godfather; a traditional token of subordination of Viking to Englishman pioneered by Alfred. Edmund was merely playing for time, however, and behind the baptismal diplomacy he was gathering an invasion force. This force descended on the disunited Vikings in 944 and drove both contenders for the northern throne back to Ireland.

At this point Edmund carried out something of a diplomatic masterstroke. He did not want to face a united coalition of northern powers as his brother had at Brunaburgh, so he granted Strathclyde to Malcolm, king of Scotland, rather than seek to annex it into England, as Athelstan had. This concession of a large, under-populated and hard to defend tract of territory won England a vital ally for fifty years, and created a vital western buffer zone against further Irish Viking invasions of northern England. Evidently a skilled diplomat, Edmund also continued Athelstan's policy of extending English influence over continental affairs – he intervened in French affairs in 945 to have his nephew, Louis IV, freed from the captivity of Duke Hugh the Great. The French

King Edmund 'the Magnificent' and his allies Malcom Canmore of Scotland (below) and Louis IV of France (bottom).

---

[129] *Anglo Saxon Chronicle*, entry for the year 942 E.H.D. Vol. 1

chronicler, Floddard, recorded that 'Edmund, king of the English, sent messengers to Duke Hugh about the restoration of King Louis, and the duke accordingly made a public agreement with his nephews and other leading men of his kingdom'.[130]

Shortly after this, in 946, Edmund died in a heroic manner, stabbed to death whilst trying to save one of his courtiers from an armed mugger called Leofa. He had reigned less than seven years, but the manner of his death, plus the fact that it coincided with victory in the long drawn out struggle for northern England caused him to be regarded by his contemporaries as one of their greatest kings, hence his later epithet 'the Magnificent'. Unfortunately, our principal contemporary source, the *Anglo-Saxon Chronicle,* barely mentions the events of his reign beyond his campaigns in the north. However we do have a surviving legal code[131] specifically directed at the destructive English tradition of the blood feud, suggesting he continued his brother's attempts to bring unity and peace to what had been a fractured, ethnically divided and violent society. This document unambiguously treats killings resulting from a blood feud: Previously it was considered an extra legal right by many English and Danes, as murder, like any other deliberate death, and subjected the perpetrators to the common law compensation code of *weregild.* More significantly still, in the last two years of his life Edmund was responsible for the appointment of England's greatest statesman of the 10th century: Dunstan.

Dunstan and the reigns of Eadred and Eadwig

Dunstan's talents had risen to royal attention through his efficient reform of Glastonbury Abbey as its Abbot. He combined a formidable personality with an astute grasp of politics and a commitment to the reform of the Church. These attributes caused him to be elevated to Edmund's royal council where he swiftly rose to pre-eminence, effectively serving as the head of royal government on from 944 until 978 with a brief exile in the 950s,

---

[130] Floddard's *Annals* entry for the year 946 transl. Whitelock D. in E.H.D. vol. 1 p. 345
[131] *Edmund's code concerning the blood feud* (II Edmund 939-946) Ibid. pp. 427-429

spanning the reigns of six monarchs.

10th century illustration of Dunstan

Dunstan and Eadred formed an effective political partnership during the latter's brief reign of 952-955. The admittedly deeply subjective hagiography the *Life of St Dunstan* proclaimed how Eadred, 'Loved the blessed Dunstan with such great warmth and love that he preferred hardly anyone of his chief men to him. And the man of God on his side was accustomed to acclaim the king dearest of all to him'[132]. However, the partnership of king and cleric faced a serious factional problem from the outset of Eadred's reign – the court dividing between a pro-reform East Anglian party and a conservative Wessex party. Dunstan, whose sympathies lay with the former, but by birth belonged to the latter, was ideal as a conciliator. Eadred was in any case unable to fulfil the role himself as in 947 half-subdued Northumbria broke out in a final round

---

[132] Anon. *Life of St Dunstan* paragraph 20 Ibid. p. 900

of rebellion. Once again instigated by Wulfstan, the duplicitous Archbishop of York, yet another Irish Viking king was acknowledged at York, the Norwegian exile Eric Bloodaxe.

Bloodaxe was a formidable warrior but an inept ruler, and within two years the Northumbrian nobility had renounced him in favour of another Norwegian, the more conciliatory Olaf Sihtricsson. Eadred, the most brutal of the Cerdicynns, decided that the time for negotiation was over. In 948 he launched a savage punitive expedition into Northumbria, its primary objective being terror as opposed to the expulsion of his enemy. He sustained a defeat at Castleford, but his threats afterwards seem to have been so terrible that at least a part of the Northumbrian nobility defected to him anyway, 'The king became so angry that he wished to march back into the land and destroy it utterly. When the councillors of the Northumbrians understood that, they deserted Eric and paid to King Eadred compensation for their act'[133].

Despite this apparent statement of surrender, another six years would elapse before Northumbria fully submitted to Eadred's rule. Eadred's decision to violate the convention that clergy were exempt from secular authority by imprisoning Archbishop Wulfstan, in 952, seems to have been crucial in achieving this, it is likely that the support of Dunstan helped shield the king from the potentially disastrous consequences of this action. With Wulfstan removed, the Northumbrian nobility appear to have become divided amongst themselves, a faction inviting Eric Bloodaxe back as king just two years later driving him out again and apparently voluntarily submitting to the rule of Eadred. Bloodaxe himself was later killed by a fellow Scandinavian Earl Macchus at Stainmore, in 954, having become something of an embarrassment to the Northumbrian nobility.

Eadred's suppression of the Bloodaxe rebellion marks the both the end of hopes for an independent Northumbria and in general the end of the pagan Viking threat to England, ushering in the longest period of peace in Anglo-

---

[133] *Anglo-Saxon Chronicle* entry for the year 948 Ibid.

Saxon history. This would only become apparent with hindsight, however, and Anglo-Saxon England continued to regard itself as a nation permanently under the threat of invasion. Eadred's will makes this clear, leaving a vast sum for the relief of the suffering caused by future Viking raids, 'He [Eadred] grants for the relief of his soul and the benefit of his people 1600 pounds, to the end that they may redeem themselves from famine and from a heathen army if they need.'[134] Nonetheless, it is a testimony to the unparalleled tranquillity prevailing in his realm in the last year of his life that Eadred felt able to release the troublesome Archbishop Wulfstan.

Eadred clearly did not inspire affection in his people. But he was respected for his astuteness, and for his fairness – he was willing to shed East Anglian blood as freely as Northumbrian when the murder of the Abbot of Thetford in 952 resulted in an exemplary slaughter. Above all, his piety and generosity, oddly contrasting with his undoubted brutality seem to have contributed towards a positive memory.

The *Anglo-Saxon Chronicle* tells us that Eadred's successor, Eadwig, was just 16 when he inherited the throne in 955. He is the first Cerdicynn ruler to garner a bad press, the hagiographer of St Dunstan describing him as 'A youth indeed in aged and endowed with little wisdom in government'.[135] The same hagiographer tells us that Dunstan discovered Eadwig in bed with his mistresses in the midst of his coronation celebrations and physically dragged him back to the feast. Unsurprisingly, Eadwig seems to have grown up with a distaste for clergy and, according to the hagiographer, drove Dunstan into temporary exile. Our evidence for his reign is very limited. The *Anglo-Saxon Chronicle* is virtually silent. However, a surviving charter granting the land of Southwell[136] to the Archdiocese of York does indicate that he preserved the traditionally open handed patronage of the Church by the Cerdicynn dynasty, at least to some extent. Nonetheless it does seem clear that by 957 Eadwig's fitness to rule was being widely questioned – in that year the Mercians and

---

[134]*Will of King Eadred* 951-55 Ibid. p. 555.
[135] *Life of St Dunstan* para 21 Ibid. p. 900.
[136] *Grant by King Eadwig of Southwell to Oscetel, Archbishop of York* (956) Charter no. 108 Ibid. p. 56.

Northumbrians openly rejected him, declaring his younger brother Edgar as their king. Quite what Eadwig's faults were is unclear, the *Life of St Dunstan* simply states that he 'Acted foolishly in the government committed to him, ruining with vain hatred the shrewd and wise, and admitting with loving zeal the ignorant and those like himself'.[137] Fortunately no invader took advantage of this rift in English government, and it was resolved in 959 by Eadwig's death and Dunstan's recall from exile by Edgar who now assumed the throne of England unchallenged.

Edgar's reign – Rule of the saints?

Of all the Cerdicynn kings, Edgar is the most neglected by historians. Presiding over a uniquely peaceful period of prosperity, his reign has often been interpreted as an uninteresting calm bracketed by the stormy reigns of England's nation builders before and the catastrophic Aethelred afterwards. Part of the challenge is assessing who was actually making policy during Edgar's reign, the king himself or Dunstan. Sources are unanimous in declaring that the pious Edgar and his Archbishop cooperated in all matters. Moreover, on his return from exile, Dunstan rapidly assembled a 'cabinet' of clerical ministers: Bishops Ælfstan of London, Oswald of Worcester and Æthelwold of Winchester. These four seem to have formed an inner circle of government around Edgar. Only 16 or 17 at the start of his reign, it is clear that the young Edgar was impressionable and allowed Dunstan to exert unchecked influence over government. Indeed William of Malmesbury tells us that Edgar was so enamoured of Dunstan's learning that he went in person to study at Glastonbury Abbey where the latter as abbot had set up an educational foundation.[138] However, even when Edgar reached maturity there is no shift in governmental policy apparent, suggesting either that he continued to be dominated by Dunstan, or that there was genuine synergy in their beliefs and policies. This is most evident in the greatest building project of Edgar's reign, the New Minster of Winchester, a vast church by Anglo-Saxon standards begun under Dunstan's auspices, but completed as a

---

[137] *Life of St Dunstan* para 24 Ibid. p. 901
[138] William of Malmesbury *Gesta regum anglorum* Book VIII Ibid.

Benedictine institution under Edgar's direction in 963. This building was intended as a statement of sacerdotal monarchy – the ornate tombs of Edgar's royal predecessors were prominently displayed in the nave in a manner designed to emphasise the divinely appointed nature of the Cerdiycnn family's legitimacy in a smooth blend of Roman imperial and Catholic liturgical traditions that Dunstan and Edgar would once again employ in his coronation ceremony of 973[139].

The exceptional union of the power of church and state in the form of Dunstan and Edgar gave rise to a systematic reform programme, aimed simultaneously at both institutions, which focussed on raising the morals of the entire nation. Dunstan believed that morality should be the first objective of good governance, for in accordance with divine justice a moral nation would perforce also become a peaceful and prosperous one. Dunstan's hagiographer succinctly summarises the intent of Dunstan and Edgar's moral crusade:

'As soon as the blessed king had been fittingly instructed in royal usage and sacred customs by the blessed Dunstan and other wise men, he began to supress evil doers everywhere, to love with a pure heart the just and virtuous, to subdue kings and tyrants on all sides, to restore or enrich the destroyed churches of God, to collect together communities serving in praise of the Supreme Godhead, and to preserve in kingly fashion his whole country with peaceful protection'[140].

---

[139] Karkov C 'The frontispieice to the New Minster Charter and the King's Two Bodies' in Ed. Scragg D *Edgar: King of the English* (Woodbridge, 2008) pp. 224-242.
[140] Anon. *Life of St Dunstan* para. 25 E.H.D. Vol I p. 902

Frontispiece to Edgar's Charter granting land to the New Minster, Winchester directly linking the pious king to the enthroned Christ.

Primarily Church reform was concerned with enforcing discipline and orthodoxy. To this end, Edgar and Dunstan imposed uniformity on English monasteries, requiring them to follow Benedictine rules as laid down in Aethelwold's *Regularis Concordia* of 973. Using the model Dunstan had established at Glastonbury Abbey, the whole English church was ruthlessly purged of corrupt individuals and practise, such as simony (the selling of church offices). Numerous new foundations were created and the existing ones enriched by gifts of land by the king and nobles of like mind. In addition a campaign was launched to restore lands formerly owned by monastic institutions but subsequently alienated by long term lease to secular landowners. As a result of these reforms and the clear pre-eminence accorded to the Benedictine order by the king, monasteries emerged as major forces in local and national government for the first time, adding a new, more organised form of Catholicism to the English, who had hitherto been served by a loose structure of minster churches largely staffed by secular, or canon, priests.

Politically, Edgar focussed on justice, issuing a new law code which took the first English national law code of Alfred the Great as its basis and developed it to reflect the reality of Edgar's much larger, more multicultural realm. This code emphasised the equality of his various subjects before the

172

law 'This measure is to be common to all the nation, whether Englishmen, Danes or Britons, in very province of my dominion, to the end that poor man and rich may possess what they rightly acquire'[141]. Indeed Edgar went further, allowing 'home rule' within the Danelaw wherein its inhabitants: 'It is my will that there should be in force among the Danes such good laws as they best decide on'[142]. Such an expansive vision produced a simple, practical code that would form the basis of English common law, before and after the Norman Conquest, for over two centuries. Elsewhere, the efficiency of Edgar's ministers, as well as their piety, can be seen in the changing language of charters – those of Edgar's predecessors had often been floral, pompous and vague in their language, Edgar's are businesslike and models of clarity, reflecting the emergence of a new professionalism amongst the clerks recruited by Dunstan and his assistants:

'I, Edgar... bestow a certain portion of land, namely 10 hides at the place which is commonly called Kineton, on my faithful thegn... Aelfwold, as an eternal inheritance... with all advantages, namely meadows, pastures, woods; and after the conclusion of his life leave it unburdened to whosoever heirs he chooses. Also the aforesaid estate is to be free from every yoke of earthly service except three, namely fixed military service and the restoration of bridges and fortresses'[143].

Edgar's law code comprises three parts: the Hundred Ordinance which is particularly concerned with the sanctity of property rights, and the Andover and Wihtbordesstan codes, which mainly address obligations in terms of service and taxation. These law codes would later establish a particularly savage reputation – William of Malmesbury in the 12th century claims that Edgar had criminals blinded, their nostrils slit, hands, feet and noses cut off and additionally scalped[144]. His surviving codes make no mention of this brutality, however, which would be out of character both for Edgar and for the

---

[141] Article 2 of Edgar's law code issued at "Wihtbordesstan" (IV Edgar 962-3) Ibid. p.435
[142] Ibid.
[143] 'Grant by King Edgar of land at Kineton, Warwickshire to his *thegn* Alefwold' (969) Charter No. 113 Ibid. p. 563
[144] William of Malmesbury *Gesta regum anglorum* Book VIII Ibid.

pattern of Cerdicynn law which was primarily based on the compensation culture of *weregild*.

Beyond law, Edgar's currency reforms also recognise the need to amend existing practise in the light of the size and complexity of the 10th century kingdom of England. The old devolved system, whereby every burgh had the right to mint its own silver pennies, with a wide degree of variation in pattern and silver content, lead to inflation and endemic forging. All of this was replaced late in Edgar's reign by what numismatists call the 'Reform Small Cross' penny, the first truly national English currency, produced using standardised, centrally manufactured dies and featuring the names of both the mint of origin and the moneyer for added accountability[145]. This system would be used to produce English currency into the 16th century and, provided the monarch did not toy with the precious metal content, produced one of the most stable currencies in Europe.

Perhaps the most interesting element of Edgar's reign was his formal coronation – a curious event in that it was held 14 years after the king inherited the English throne and only two years before Edgar's death. William of Malmesbury claims the extended delay was the result of a penance placed upon Edgar by Dunstan for having killed a rival in love for the hand of his future queen, Ælfthryth[146] . This theory has been rejected by later historians as mere romance, however, the balance of opinion being that this coronation represents the *culmination* of Edgar's reign as opposed to its start. Starkey, in particular, believes that the coronation was a carefully stage-managed piece of dynastic propaganda, authored by Dunstan to formalise the position Edgar by virtue of the conquests and nation building of his predecessors: 'He was to be anointed king of the English; honoured as emperor of Britain, and revered as a second Christ'.[147]

The details of the coronation ceremony devised by Dunstan certainly

---

[145] Pagan H. 'The Pre-Reform Coinage of Edgar' in Ed. Scragg D. *Edgar: King of the English* (Woodbridge, 2008) p. 192.
[146] Ibid.
[147] Starkey (2003) p. 74

support this idea of the king being recognised as a ruler appointed by God as well as by rightful succession. From the Germanic tradition of his forefathers Edmund received the ring and sword of kingship, from the biblical tradition of Solomon and David he received a crown (previous Anglo-Saxon kings had been crowned with a *cunehelm* or royal helmet), sceptre and rod whilst from the Roman tradition came a laurel diadem and the choice of setting – Bath, site of the most impressive surviving Roman buildings in England.

This heady symbolism was capped by the choice of date, which equated Edgar's rule to that of Christ Himself: 'Great joy had come to all on that blessed day which the children of men call... Pentecost... then had passed from the birth of the glorious King [Jesus], the Guardian of light, ten hundred years reckoned in numbers.'[148] A final act of imperial pretension followed shortly afterwards: Edgar was rowed across the River Dee at Chester by independent Welsh and Scottish monarchs who, in an act of submission, had acknowledged him to be their overlord.

Edgar's journey across the Dee represents the climax of the Cerdicynn dynasty. At this moment they wielded authority unmatched since the days of Rome. Edgar's deliberate cultivation of the comparison is clear in his currency, which very obviously imitates the Roman style, even to the point of ornamenting his profiled head with a crown clearly copied from that of the emperors. Documents from Edgar's reign have a self-confident permanence in their tone, that speaks of a regime thoroughly secure in its authority, Article 1.6 of Edgar's law code of 962-3, concerning payment of taxes to the Church declares: 'It is my will that these dues of God shall be alike everywhere in my dominion'[149].

Ironically, even as this law code was being written, Edgar and Dunstan were laying down the foundations of a policy that would shatter the stability of the Cerdicynn throne – monastic land endowment. Under the influence of his Archbishop, Edgar was an exceptionally generous patron to monasteries,

---

[148] *Anglo-Saxon Chronicle* entry for the year 228 E.H.D. Vol. 1 p. 228
[149] Article 1.6 of Edgar's Law code Ibid. p. 435

indeed William of Malmesbury directly equated Edgar's policy of yearly endowments of new monasteries with securing God's favour and with it peace for England[150]. Such a policy did not secure his nobles' favour, however. So extensive was the transfer of land to monasteries under Edgar that it threatened the whole social order of the shire system – the previously dominant position of the *ealdormen* being threatened by the rising power of the abbots of wealthy monasteries. Opponents of this policy were not confined to the secular nobility either. There is evidence of church land being redistributed from secular priests to monasteries too, land which had hitherto been regarded as hereditary livings for priests who often came from the same noble families as the *ealdormen*. A contemporary account, attributed to Bishop Aethelwold, states, 'Assuredly he drove out canons who abounded beyond measure in the foresaid sins, and he established monks in all the foremost places of all his dominion.'[151] As long as Edgar lived, his authority, combined with that of the formidable Dunstan, seems to have been sufficient to prevent dissent spilling over into rebellion. However, after Edgar's death in 975, this divisive policy swiftly resulted in the emergence of political factions, with catastrophic consequences for the government of England.

The coronation stone of Kingston-upon-Thames, the traditional site of the crowning of English kings in the 10th century

---

[150] William of Malmesbury Chapter 8 Ibid.
[151] Attrib. Aethelwold 'An Old English account of King Edgar's establishment of monasteries' (975-984) Ibid. p.921.

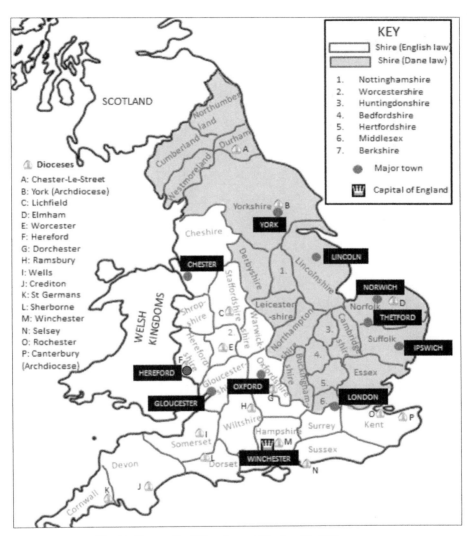

SCOTLAND

Northumberland

Cumberland
Westmoreland
Durham
A

♜ Dioceses

A: Chester-Le-Street
B: York (Archdiocese)
C: Lichfield
D: Elmham
E: Worcester
F: Hereford
G: Dorchester
H: Ramsbury
I: Wells
J: Crediton
K: St Germans
L: Sherborne
M: Winchester
N: Selsey
O: Rochester
P: Canterbury
(Archdiocese)

Yorkshire ♜ B

YORK

Cheshire

Derbyshire

Lincolnshire

LINCOLN

CHESTER

Shrop-shire

Staffordshire

1.

Warwickshire

Leicester-shire

C ♜

2.

Northamptonshire

3.

Cambridgeshire

NORWICH
Norfolk ♜ D

THETFORD

WELSH KINGDOMS

Hereford-shire

F ♜ E

Suffolk

IPSWICH

HEREFORD

Gloucester-shire

Oxfordshire

Buckinghamshire

4.

Essex

OXFORD

G

5.

LONDON

GLOUCESTER

H ♜

6.

O ♜ ♜ P

Wiltshire

Surrey

Kent

♜ I

Somerset

Hampshire

♛ ♜ M

Sussex

L ♜

Dorset

WINCHESTER

♜ N

Devon

J ♜

Cornwall K ♜

Fig 13: The unified Kingdom of England in 975

177

Historiography

Medieval:

The Anglo-Saxon Chronicle

Life of St Dunstan

Attrib. Aethelwold *An Old English account of King Edgar's establishment of monasteries*

Floddard *Annals*

William of Malmesbury *Gesta regum anglorum*

Current debate:

David Starkey in *The Monarchy of England Volume 1: Beginnings* (Chatto and Windus, London, 2004) p. 73 argues for a forceful imposition of the structures and culture of Wessex over the rest of the English people – the new state of England was essentially 'Greater Wessex'. In this they were aided by the Church to whom they were generous benefactors and in particular the Archbishop of Canterbury Dunstan.

Sir Frank Stenton in *Anglo-Saxon England* (Oxford University Press, 1971) disputes the notion of a 'Wessex hegemony' in the 10th century, arguing that with the exception of a lull in the period 955-980 the period was essentially one of ongoing rivalry and strife between Anglo-Saxons and Vikings manifested in rebellions and invasions.

In the BBC television series *Alfred the Great and the Anglo-Saxons* (first broadcast 2014) Michael Wood argues for a heightened role for Alfred's daughter, Aethelflaed 'the Lady of the Mercians', in the creation of England. He believes she acted as an essential bridge between the nation building ambitions of the Cerdicynn dynasty and the independent spirit of the Mericans who traditionally viewed Wessex as their rival and enemy.

Sarah Foot in *Athelstan: The First King of England* (Yale University Press 2011) argues that Athelstan deserves to be seen as more than simply a consolidator of the conquests of his father, Edward, and grandfather, Alfred. He was, she believes, the first ruler to visualise Britain as opposed to England as a political entity and his polices in the aftermath of the decisive Battle of Brunaburgh in 935 are those of a monarch determined to extend the notion of the nation state to encompass the Celtic as well as English peoples of the island of Britain.

Questions to consider

- To what extent were Edward the Elder's achievements due to his sister Aethelflead?

- How far was Athelstan's success in uniting England based on the achievements of Edward the Elder?

- 'More than just a successful war lord.' Assess this view of Aethelstan.

- To what extent can Edmund be viewed as the first true king of a united England?

- 'Aethelstan was a more successful ruler than Edgar.' Discuss.

- 'Dunstan was effectively king of England in the reigns of Eadred, Eadwig and Edgar'. Discuss.

- Assess the political and religious importance of the reign of Edgar.

Chapter 10: Edward and Aethelred – Decline and Fall

Aethelred's nemesis: Sven Forkbeard king of Denmark, Norway and ultimately England too. Illustration from a 13th century manuscript.

The last Cerdicynn kings

Edward 'the Martyr' 975: Murdered by his stepmother

Athelred 'the Unready' 975-1013, 1013-1015: Overthrown by the Danish dynasty of Sven Forkbeard

Key dates

978: Murder of Edward leads to Dunstan's retirement from public life

981: Renewed Viking attacks on England

991: Pyrrhic Viking victory at Maldon marks beginning of terminal decay of Cerdicynn dynasty

994: Sven Forkbeard besieges London

1001: Ealdorman Pallig of the Danelaw defects to Sven Forkbeard

1002: St Brice's Day Massacre, collapse of Aethelred's authority

The regicide of Edward and the collapse of consensus

'In this year King Edward was killed at the gap of Corfe on 18 March in the evening, and he was buried at Wareham without any royal honours. And no worse deed than this for the English people was committed since first they came to Britain. Men murdered him, but God honoured him. In life he was an earthly king; he is now after death a heavenly saint'[152].

The habitually drily and factual *Anglo-Saxon Chronicle's* glowing hagiography of Edward the Martyr stands testimony to the contemporary outrage his murder caused in the Anglo-Saxon world – a *cause célèbre* as infamous in its time as the assassination of John F. Kennedy in our own. As boys of about thirteen and nine respectively, neither Edward, nor Aethelred who succeeded him, had any role in the events of 979. Rather they were tools in a factional dispute that had its roots in the later years of Edgar's reign.

Edgar and Dunstan's policy of wholesale transfer of land to monastic institutions led to the formation of a faction of *ealdormen* in court determined to maintain their traditional domination of landownership in the shires. The leadership of this faction were three *Ealdormen*, Aelfhere, Aethlwold and Ordgar. Between them these *Ealdormen* controlled much of Mercia, western England and East Anglia. They were also closely related to Edgar's third and final queen, Ælfthryth, the mother of Edgar's youngest son, *aethling* Aethelred. Facing them was a pro-monastic faction, headed by Dunstan, but also including loyalist ealdormen, such as Byrthnoth of Essex. They favoured Edgar's eldest son, the *atheling* Edward whose mother was Edgar's first wife Æthelflæd, 'the white duck'. Normally the combination of Edward's seniority plus the support of the foremost clergyman and politician in England would have been sufficient to make Edward's claim unassailable. There were, however, doubts as to his legitimacy as his parents had been lovers for many years before they were married.

In the short term, legitimacy qualms could not prevail against Dunstan's

---

[152] *Anglo-Saxon Chronicle* entry for the year 979 in E.H.D. Vol. 1

will, and Edward was duly crowned. If the anonymous hagiographer of St Oswald is to be believed, however, the teenage Edward's repellent personality swiftly antagonised the court; apparently he 'Inspired in all not only fear but even terror, for [he scoured them] not only with words but truly with dire blows.'[153] Whether this is true or not, the likelihood of the young king falling under the dominance of Dunstan's monastic faction drove their opponents to desperate lengths.

Accordingly, at Corfe in Dorset on 18 March 978, Edward, who was visiting his stepmother and stepbrother, Ælfthryth and Aethelred was set upon by the latter's *thegns*, stabbed to death and unceremoniously buried at nearby Wareham. To add to the insult to contemporary sensibilities, nobody was tried for the crime, clearly hinting at the complicity of *Ealdorman* Aelfhere and Ælfthryth herself, who swiftly established themselves at the head of a regency government which rapidly elevated Aethelred to the throne.

Whatever his faults in life, in death Edward the Martyr, as he became known, was swiftly canonised and became the object of a cult of veneration, his devotees including a clearly guilt ridden Aethelred. Even Aelfhere, perhaps moved by public opinion, was persuaded to perform an act of contrition, removing Edward's body from its makeshift burial in Wareham and reburying it in state near Shaftesbury – the surviving Anglo-Saxon church of St Lawrence in Bradford-on-Avon may well have been its final resting place.

The Church of St Lawrence, Bradford-upon-Avon built circa 1000. A high status building, it may be the reliquary chapel of Edward the Martyr.

[153] Anon *Life of St Oswald, Archbishop of York* No. 236 Ibid. p

Aethelred's reign

Aethelred was clearly innocent of the murder of his step-brother. However, to the superstitious Anglo-Saxons, a reign which was founded on such infamy was likely to be doomed from the start. Significantly the *Anglo-Saxon Chronicle* records a portent in the sky similar to that seen before the first Viking raids, 'A bloody cloud was often seen in the likeness of fire, and especially it was revealed at midnight, and it was formed in various shafts of light'. [154] Despite this, the first two years of Aethelred's reign were peaceful enough. Dunstan seems to have quietly accepted the seizure of power by Aelfhere and his faction, retiring to Canterbury for the remainder of his life, an action which effectively decapitated the pro-monastic party in government.

An early 13th century illustration of Aethelred the Unready.

However, in 980 the Vikings returned. The new Viking threat was radically different from that which had confronted Alfred. Denmark had been transformed by the visionary king, Harold Bluetooth, in the early 10th century along the English model into a well organised, disciplined nation state with a national army based around a series of fortified camps known as *trelleborgs*. He was also responsible for the conversion of his realm to Christianity. Accordingly, the raids that he and his son and successor Sven Forkbeard unleashed on England were on a larger scale, more disciplined and more systematic than those of a century earlier. Specifically these raids targeted population centres and military installations such as burghs and harbours, rather than Christian sites, the intention being to spread terror and progressively wear down the formidable English defences. The raid of 980, for example, featured a coordinated attack on Thanet in Kent, Cheshire and the Royal Navy's dockyard at Southampton.

---

[154] *Anglo-Saxon Chronicle* entry for the year 979 Ibid. p.231

The peace of Edgar's reign had made the English elite complacent. Defences had been neglected. For example, the Royal Navy had largely been laid up out of service to save money. Moreover, the shire *ealdormen*, the core of the English command structure, were largely elderly and for the most part died within ten years of Athelred's accession. Their replacements had little experience of war and hence were consistently outmanoeuvred by the battle hardened Danish Vikings, who either surprised and destroyed them, such as the Somerset *fyrd* at Watchet in 989, or, if they deemed them too strong, evaded them altogether, as they did against Aethelred and his field army in 1000.

Anglo-Saxon reliquary cross made in the reign of Aethelred the Unready, a testament to the vibrancy of 10th century English culture even in the midst of renewed Viking invasion.

In the midst of these disasters, Aethelred quietly came of age, assuming direct control of the realm around 984 following the death of Athelwold, Bishop of Worcester, who seems to have served as both guardian and chief minister. The new king appears hesitant and eager to please, as opposed to incompetent during this first phase of his reign, as is shown by the apparently contradictory nature of his policies – a charter of 993 restored the privileges of Abingdon Abbey, but he also allowed his thegn, Æthelsige, to seize land belonging to Rochester diocese in 984. At the moment when England needed strong leadership to meet a threat of a magnitude unmatched for a century, what it got was a hesitant, inexperienced king who trusted courtiers who put their own self-interest before the nation's.

Despite this, the heroic action of the veteran *Ealdorman,* Brythnoth of Essex, at the Battle of Maldon in 991 might have served as a rallying point for resistance, had Aethelred chosen to take it. After a tense stand-off across a flooded creek, the badly outnumbered Essex *fyrd* were engaged by a Viking force, who, though they triumphed, sustained such heavy casualties that they were compelled to withdraw. Despite it being a defeat, Maldon was widely celebrated as the epitome of English heroism, in the same manner as the

Dunkirk evacuations in World War Two. Out of this publicity came the most famous battle poem in Old English, *The Battle of Maldon,* in which the author puts a positively Churchillian speech of defiance to the Danish emissary into Brythnoth's mouth:

'Hear you sea rover, what this folk says? For]tribute they will give you spears, poisoned point and ancient sword, such war gear as will profit you little in the battle. Messenger of the seaman, take back a message... how that there stands here with his troop an Ealdorman of unstained renown, who is ready to guard this realm, this home of Aethelred my lord, people and land; it is the heathen that shall fall in this battle... Not easily shall you win tribute; peace must be made with point and edge, with grim battle pay, before we give tribute'.[155]

A modern statue of Brythnoth still stands guard over Maldon.

England then was not lacking loyalty to the Cerdicynn dynasty, nor resilience in the face of aggression. In common with all medieval kingdoms, however, its weakness was that it was only as strong as the man leading it, and Aethelred's policies, from Maldon onwards, towards the Vikings could scarcely have been more ill advised; hence his nickname 'Unraed', which to his contemporaries meant 'badly advised' rather than 'Unready'. Foremost of his *unraed* counsellors was the Archbishop of Canterbury, Sigeric, who advised Aethelred to buy off the Danish invaders, despite their recent wastage at Maldon. An unprecedented sum of £22,000 was offered as *danegeld,* essentially protection money. Unsurprisingly over the next few years Svein and his commanders returned, making raid after raid, knowing that the mere threat of Viking aggression was sufficient to extract huge amounts of cash from Aethelred and his timid council, so much so that far more pennies from Aethelred's reign have been found in Denmark than England.

---

[155] Anon. *The Battle of Maldon* Ibid. p.320

The *Anglo-Saxon Chronicle* is extremely detailed in its description of the desperate years that followed Maldon. The previously formidable national defences of England appear either helpless or inept in the face of Sven's efficient attacks. The problem seems less to have been a general collapse in the national institutions, the *fyrd,* for instance, could and did inflict localised defeats on Viking raiding parties. The problem was Aethelred's curious reluctance to command the war effort in person as his predecessors had done. In his 38 year reign he only took personal command of his forces three times – 1000, 1009 and 1014. Otherwise he left command to his favoured senior *ealdormen,* such as Eadric Streona, who lacked both the acumen and authority to effectively coordinate a war effort. The result was a deeply frustrating failure to bring England's superior resources decisively into action, as the *Anglo-Saxon Chronicle's* entry for 999 records:

'In this year the [Viking] army came again round into the Thames and turned up the Medway and to Rochester. And the Kentish *fyrd* came up against them there, and joined battle stoutly; but alas! They to soon turned and fled because they did not have the support they should have had... Then the king and his councillors determined that they should be opposed by a naval force and also by a land force... And as ever, as things should have been moving, they were more delayed from one hour to the next, and ever they let their enemies' force increase, and ever the English retreated inland and the Danes continually followed; and then in the end it effected nothing'.[156]

Ravaged by raiding, impoverished by continuous extortion, England, formerly the richest country in western Europe, spiralled into economic crisis, so much so that even the traditional offering to the papacy known as Peter's Pence ceased. Indeed her troubles became the talk of Europe, a chronicler from the Holy Roman Empire recording:

'I have heard that the English... have very often suffered indescribable misery from Svein... the fierce king of the Danes, and have been driven to such a pass that they, who were formerly payers of tribute to Peter, Prince of the Apostles...

---

[156] *Anglo-Saxon Chronicle* entry for the year 999 Ibid.

have paid to unclean dogs the tribute yearly imposed upon them, and have unwillingly relinquished the greater part of their kingdom... for it to be boldly inhabited by the enemy'[157].

Despite this appalling situation, Aethelred seems to have been remarkably successful in retaining the faith and loyalty of his people, up to the end of the first millennium; evidence of how loyalty to the Cerdicynns had been embedded in the English psyche during the prosperous years of the mid-10th century. In 994, for example, a determined Viking siege of London was defeated by the spirited defence of its inhabitants who refused to renounce their loyalty to Aethelred. The only major defector to Svein's side during this period was Eadric Steona, whom, with typically poor judgement, Aethelred had elevated to the rank of *Ealdorman* of Mercia shortly before he betrayed the king. This residual loyalty perhaps explains why Sven Forkbeard initially refrained from full scale invasion.

The St Bride's Day Massacre – the end of Anglo-Saxon England

An apparently badly advised, but well intentioned Aethelred had thus far therefore kept his throne. Tragically, the frustrations of constant Viking raids brought the latent vicious streak that existed within Aethelred to the surface. Until 1001 the Danish inhabitants of England had been remarkably steadfast in their loyalty to the Cerdicynns, even in the face of their own countrymen's aggression. In that year, however, the Danish *Ealdorman* of Devon, Palig, appears to have given up hope and defected to Sven with a sizeable force of ships. Aethelred's reaction was one of the most brutal acts in English history, the St Bride's day massacre. It comprised a state organised program of the innocent civilian Danish population of England, an act comparable to the French massacre of their Huguenot population on St Bartholomew's day in 1662 or the 1990s 'ethnic cleansing' of Bosnian Moslems by their Serbian neighbours. A charter granted by Aethelred to St Frideswide's monastery in Oxford two years later attempts to justify his actions and gives an insight into

---

[157] Thietmar of Merseburg *Chronicle* No. 27 Ibid. p.347

the terrors inflicted on the Danes by their former neighbours on 13 November 1002:

"The Danes who had sprung up in this island, sprouting like cockle amongst wheat, were to be destroyed by a most just extermination, and this decree was to be put into effect even as far as death, those Danes who dwelt in Oxford striving to escape death entered [a church] and resolved to make a refuge and defence for themselves therein... when all the people in pursuit strove, forced by necessity, to drive them out, and could not, they set fire to the planks and burnt, as it seems, this church with its ornaments and its books'[158].

By the time this charter was released, Aethelred's fragile authority had collapsed. It is doubtful that the Danish Vikings would have let the royally sanctioned 'just extermination' of their kin in England go unpunished in any case, but the single act of the slaughter of Sven Forkbeard's sister, Gunnhild, wife of Ealdorman Palig, during the massacre changed the whole character of the Viking threat. In accordance with both Danish and English custom, Sven declared a blood feud against Aethelred, vowing not to rest until the latter had been dethroned.

Henceforth the whole character of the war changed. Raids were still mounted, not for pure profit now but with the aim of weakening England at strategically significant points and reconnoitring invasion routes. Aethelred seems to have retreated into a fantasy world in which his rule was still acknowledged – the first few years of the 11th century saw a flurry of new charters and even a law code released. In reality England was effectively leaderless, torn along ethnic lines and increasingly dividing into smaller sub divisions, split by no-man's lands along which the invaders moved unchecked – a situation not unlike the one the original Anglo-Saxon settlers encountered in post-Roman Britain. To all intents and purposes, therefore, Aethelred's rule,

---

[158] Renewal by King Ethelred for the monastery of St Frideswide, Oxford, of a privilege for their lands at Winchendon, Buckinghamshire, and Whitehill, Cowley and Cutslow in Oxfordshire after their church and title deeds had been burnt down during the massacre of the Danes (7 December 1004) Charter No: 127 Ibid. pp. 590-92.

and with it the Anglo-Saxon age, comes to a sad end in 1002. Thereafter, although Aethelred might still wear the crown, his fall was only a matter of time. Indeed, when Sven Forkbeard finally completed his conquests of England in 1013, many of the war ravaged inhabitants must have greeted the news with relief.

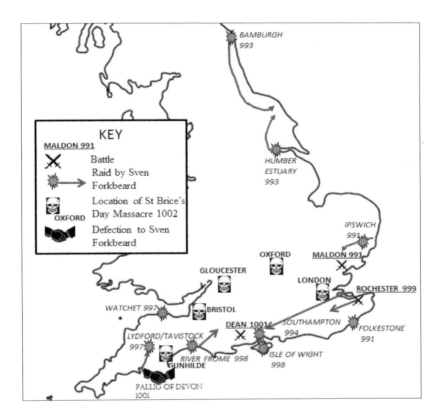

Fig. 14 The fall of Anglo-Saxon England 991-1002

Historiography

Medieval

The Anglo-Saxon Chronicle

Encomium Emmae Reginae

Florence of Worcester's *Chronicle of Chronicles*

Current debate

Anne Williams, in *Aethelread the Unready – the Ill-counselled king* (London, 2003) believes that whilst Aethelred's reign was undoubtedly catastrophic in its failure to stem the Viking invasions, this failure should not be solely attributed to Aethelred and his counsellors. Rather she argues, the system of government he inherited was systemically vulnerable to the withering effects of the economic warfare waged upon it in the late 10th and early 11th centuries. She also argues that Aethelred's judgement was inconsistent, as opposed to universally bad, with some important reforms to the shire system in particular being achieved early in his reign[159].

Eric John's view[160] is even more positive. The devastating Viking raids, he argues, were coincidental to Aethelred's policies, being derived from the *Trelleborg* military reforms of late 10th century Denmark, which would have severely taxed any English king, regardless of ability. He points to successful diplomatic efforts on Aethelred's part, for instance, negotiating a treaty with Normandy to deny the Danes its use as a raiding base, and argues the principle reason for the ineffective English response was in fact the uniquely inept and duplicitous senior nobility, whom Aethelred was compelled to rely upon, above all Edric Streona of Mercia.

---

[159] Williams A. *Aethelread the Unready – the Ill-counselled king* (London, 2003) p. 151-53
[160] John E. 'The Return of the Vikings' in Ed. Campbell J. *The Anglo-Saxons* (London, 1991) pp. 193-99.

Stenton[161] presents the view that Aethelred's weakness was the result of his brother's murder. Inheriting the throne in such inauspicious circumstances, he argues, fatally weakened the instinctive loyalty between king and people that his predecessors enjoyed. Aethelred, Stenton believes, was a weak king because he was unsure of his own power, hence his timidity in war interspersed with spasmodic bouts of violence.

Humble[162] presents the traditional view, as advanced by the *Anglo-Saxon Chronicle* that Aethelred's ineffective policies were the principle cause of England's inability to resist the Danish invasions of his reign. In particular, Humble suggests Aethelred's atrocious judgement in appointing inept advisors and unleashing ethnic violence against the peaceful Danish population settled in England sealed his dynasty's fate.

Questions to consider

- 'Aethelred's reign was doomed from the start by the murder of his brother Edward.' Discuss.
- How justified is the view that Ethelred II was personally responsible for the failure of the English to prevent Danish conquests during his reign?
- How convincing is the argument that the Danish conquest of England (c. 980– c. 1002) could not have been prevented?
- How convincing is the view that the successful renewal of Viking incursions from c.980 to c.1002 owed more to Danish strengths than to English weaknesses?

---

[161] Stenton (1987) pp. 373-74
[162] Humble (1980) pp.143-44

Chapter 11: The Anglo-Saxon legacy and the long conquest

Anglo-Saxon England did not die suddenly. Its passing as a political entity was a long drawn out affair. The very longevity of the struggle bears testimony to the latent strength of the nation the Cerdicynns and their predecessors had built and of the desirability of possessing its wealthy and efficiently run shires. This positive background should not detract from the fact that its passing was a long drawn out and deeply painful process for its inhabitants.

The death of Sven Forkbeard in 1014 triggered a confused period of civil war in which Aethelred, and his altogether more impressive son Edmund Ironside, regained a measure of authority in competition with Sven's son, Canute. The deaths of Aethelred in 1015 and Edmund in 1016 finally cleared the way for an uncontested Danish rule over England.

Edward the Confessor enthroned on the Bayeux Tapestry.

The reigns of Canute and his sons, Harold Harefoot and Harthacanute, from 1016-42, were relatively gentle – English institutions and property rights were preserved under a Danish system of overlords – the Earls. Many English in fact profited greatly from strong, peaceful rule and the opportunity to trade within Canute's Scandanavian empire. The premature deaths of Canute's sons, however, prompted a successional crisis in Denmark that resulted in the seizure of power by one last Cerdicynn King, Edward the Confessor, son of Aethelred and his second wife, Emma of Normandy.

Although a great survivor, Edward's substantial reign of 1042-1066 always had an sense of impermanence about it, caused by his failure to produce any heirs. By his death no less than four potential heirs had emerged – the only surviving male, Cerdicynn, Edmund Ironsides' teenage grandson, Edgar the *Aethling*; Harold Godwinson, senior English noble and the choice of the *witan*; the Norwegian Harald Hadrada who claimed succession via Canute; and William, Duke of Normandy, whose extremely distant matrilineal connection to Edward was boosted by the latter's apparent promise to leave the throne to him.

The death of King Harold Godwinson at the Battle of Hastings in 1066 – the moment Anglo-Saxon England died. Detail from the Bayeux Tapestry.

The fateful events of 1066 that followed are well known, as is the strong, but extremely harsh rule of William of Normandy and his son William Rufus which followed. By the death of Rufus in 1100, England was at first sight seemed unrecognisable from its Anglo-Saxon form:

- The English political and religious elite had to a man been replaced by the Normans and their allies, rebellion had been ruthlessly snuffed out of existence by 1072

- An extremely rigorous form of feudalism had swept away old property laws
- The language of English had fallen out of favour – the new Norman elite spoke a form of French, whilst the language of government and culture was now Latin, unravelling the *kulturkampf* of Alfred.

All that remained was a diminishing memory of past freedoms preserved by a colony of English noble exiles who had gained sanctuary in Constantinople, and amongst the peasantry of England, who were racially subjugated in the manner of 20th century apartheid.

If that were the whole story then Anglo-Saxon England's legacy would be brief indeed. But, even in the reign of the first two Norman kings, the essential structure of the Anglo-Saxon state survived. And thrived even, for it was far superior to anything the Normans possessed in their native land. Under Norman overlordship the shire, borough and hundred systems that formed the bedrock of local government were preserved; in a modified form much of it survives to the present. So too did the English common law system, with its emphasis on precedent. So too did the institutions of central government, rule by writ and a governing council of bishops and regional aristocrats, renamed from *witangameot* to *Curia Regis*. Even the *herthweru* military system of the English kings and their lords survived within the feudal system, the Normans renaming them their *familia*.

Simple adaptation of existing custom became something more sophisticated under Henry I, who inherited the throne in 1100.

A Victorian engraving of Edith of Scotland. Henry I's marriage to her reintroduced Cerdicynn royal blood to the English succession.

194

The early measures of his reign indicate that the nation state of England, as well as its institutions, had survived the conquests of the 11th century. Within a year of inheriting the throne, Henry repudiated the tyrannies of his brother and father, pledging to rule in accordance with the laws and customs of Edward the Confessor, an action in part motivated by Henry's own sense of justice, but undoubtedly also determined by an awareness that the English had too strong a sense of self to be obliterated as a people, a legacy of the nation building measures of Alfred and his successors. Moved by the same sentiments, Henry married one of the last Cerdicynns, Edith of Scotland, and through her re-introduced a notion of legitimate rule to his English subjects. Their intermingled Norman and English blood would ultimately give rise to the Plantagenets, England's longest ruling dynasty through whom Britain's current royal family can trace its lineage back to the Cerdicynns.

The robustness of the English notion of nationhood and identity can be seen by the survival of English despite a 300 year period of neglect. In the late 14th century court of Edward III, the poet Geoffrey Chaucer pioneered the revival of English as a language of culture, and by the 15th it was once again the language of the governing classes, part of a general erosion of the distinction between Norman and English from the reign of Henry I onwards. It has never lost its pre-eminent position, and indeed gained the unique distinction in the 20th century of evolving into England's greatest export, the first truly global language.

Geoffrey Chaucer, 'the father of English Literature' and author of 'The Canterbury Tales'

It is clearly romanticising to suggest that the Anglo-Saxons were the origin of all the institutions, traditions and beliefs that created modern Britain.

195

Many of the most defining features of the modern country developed in the later medieval period, such as parliament, or later still, such as the very notion of democracy. Overwhelmingly rural, sparsely populated early medieval Britain is clearly an alien world compared to today's urbanised state. But it is equally false to suggest a sharp break or 'year zero' moment in the development of the country with the Norman invasion of 1066.

From the moment Northumbria emerges in the early 7th century as the first politically coherent post-Roman state in Britain the process of English state building begins. Through the rise and fall of the heptarchy in the later 7th and 8th century we see the process of state building spread throughout the English realms. Thanks to the greatest ruler of the early medieval period, Alfred, this process survives its moment of greatest peril in the form of Viking invasion, emerging in a stronger and more sophisticated form as 'England' - a unique example of a 10th century politically, socially and culturally unified nation state. Anglo-Saxon England was thus the first place to undergo the ongoing process of political and cultural self-awareness that continues to unfold across the world to the present, making new nation states as it does so. Its brief golden age under the Cerdicynns of the 10th century provided sufficient time for the idea of England as a coherent identity to bed down and acquire permanence. It is this sense of nationhood, indeed the very concept of it, built upon by later medieval kings and indeed rulers ever since which perhaps forms the Anglo-Saxons' most enduring legacy, along with their prodigiously adaptable language.

In the 20th and 21st century just enough evidence has survived from the Anglo-Saxon period for us to understand them as the originators of this ongoing national process of evolution. Fascinatingly, the educated amongst them, schooled in the postclassical tradition of *exigesis*, glimpsed this themselves. Through their words and intentions we can see a view of the world startlingly aware of their part in its future, from the unique *Anglo-Saxon Chronicle*, conceived from the outset as a continuously updating record in the manner of a medieval website, to the words of Bede, directly addressing his audience in the distant future:

'I humbly entreat the reader, that if he shall find anything in these our writings anything not delivered according to the truth, he will not lay the blame on me for, as the true rule of history requires, withholding nothing, I have laboured to commit to writing such things as I could gather from common report, for the instruction of posterity'[163].

---

[163] Bede Preface to *Ecclesiastical History*

Chapter 12: A Benighted Age? The Historiography of Anglo-Saxon England

Ever since 1066, the Anglo-Saxon period has been considered from two opposing poles:

- That it was a barbaric, regressive interval between Roman and Norman civilisation – the 'Dark Ages'.
- The other, currently more favoured, model that, as 'the early medieval' period, the 500 years of Anglo-Saxon dominance in Britain represents a time of both decline and growth, and integral part of the British historical narrative, building on the post classical world it inherited and laying down foundations for the post-Norman Conquest world which succeeded it, not least the language it left behind it.

Anglo-Saxon historiography – extent and survival

Prior to the Northumbrian Renaissance of the 7th century, it is impossible to write history as we would recognise it of the Anglo-Saxon period, i.e. principally based on written sources. Between the fall of the Roman Empire in Britain in 410 and the founding of the scholar monasteries of Northumbria in 674, our contemporary written evidence is both tiny and fragmentary, making this pre-heptarchic or 'migratory' period of English history a true 'Dark Age', accessible principally through folk memory, such as the legend of Arthur and more usefully through its archaeological footprint. It is the tradition Bede re-founded of objective, chronologically ordered recording of historical fact that enables us to study the Anglo-Saxon period as historians – truly he is 'the father of British history'.

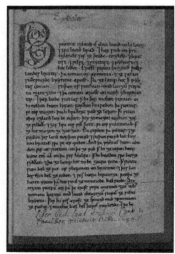

The Peterborough manuscript of the *Anglo-Saxon Chronicle*, now in the Parker Library, Corpus Christi College, Cambridge

Bede's legacy came perilously close to destruction in the 16th century, however. The printing press postdates the Anglo-Saxon period by four hundred years and as such all records were hand written in limited quantities and usually preserved in the monasteries they were written in. The wanton destruction of monastic libraries during the Henrician Reformation of the 1530s undoubtedly led to the permanent disappearance of many records of this period of history. Those that survived did so through the intercession of Tudor antiquarians, such as Elizabethan Archbishop Matthew Parker, who saved what were often the sole surviving copies of manuscripts in their private collections[164]. A case in point is our principle contemporary source for the reign of Alfred, Asser, whose biography has come down to us via a single copy that was salvaged by Henrician antiquarian, John Leland, subsequently passed to the Parker Library and printed in 1722; fortuitous as the original was destroyed in a fire just a few years later[165].

Matthew Parker, Elizabethan Archbishop and saviour of Anglo-Saxon antiquarianism.

Copy of the first page of Asser's *Life of Alfred* made in 1721 prior to its destruction in a fire in 1730.

[164] Parker's library of medieval manuscripts survives today at Corpus Christi College Cambridge. The entire collection has been put online at www.parkerweb.stanford.edu.
[165] Keynes S. and Lapidge M. 'Notes on Asser's Life of King Alfred' in Ed. Keynes S. and Lapidge M. (London, 2004) pp. 23-4

What we have left from the era, therefore, is an adequate, but strictly limited array of primary evidence, presenting the historian with plentiful challenges in corroborating material and assessing their typicality. Mercia, in particular, suffers in this regard, as it lacked a state historian of the order of Bede or Asser. Therefore we have to make use of often very oblique references to the affairs of the kingdom from a very diverse range of sources, European as well as English, many of which, such as the prolific Alcuin of York, recorded the events of their time not out of a desire to preserve objective fact, but to use them as case studies for theological arguments. Despite, in fact, because of these limitations, study of the Anglo-Saxon period is both fascinating in its challenges and exceptionally egalitarian in that the full, limited pool of evidence may be made available to all scholars of the period, whether at school, university or at the forefront of research, in a way that later periods cannot; the sheer mass of evidence requiring filtering and selection by academics to make it at all digestible to a wider audience.

Our written evidence from the Anglo-Saxon period comes in two forms – preserved primary documents, such as charters and laws, and contemporary histories. Almost without exception, they were the work of clergy and monks, the literate class of the era – Alfred stands alone in this period as a literate king who wrote his own books. Apart from Bede, none of these individuals claimed to be historians. Indeed the profession did not exist in its modern form until the 19th century. Rather they recorded the past as an integral element of the universal purpose of medieval learning – the revealing of God's plan for humanity. As a result, these historians, or 'chroniclers' as they refer to themselves, deliberately blend historical evidence with wider musings on philosophy and theology, and often give disproportionate attention to small events or anecdotes as a means of illustrating some wider point. The *Anglo-Saxon Chronicle,* for instance, devotes four lines to the omens that appeared in the sky in 793, warning of the first Viking raid on Northumbria, but only one line on the raid itself[166]. They are, moreover, naturally inclined to give a pro- Church slant to their interpretation of events. On the plus side, the best

---

[166] *Anglo-Saxon Chronicle* entry for the year 794 E.H.D. Vol. 1

of them are remarkably scrupulous in their handling of evidence. In a world where God intervened in every event, deliberate distortion of what had transpired was looked upon as a sin. Hence Bede's careful explanation of the sources of his *Ecclesiastical History*: 'the writings of the ancients, or the traditions of our forefathers, or of my own knowledge'.[167]

The contribution of Bede has already been discussed in Chapter 4. Between Bede and the reign of Alfred we have an unfortunate hiatus in historical writing in which only the tentatively dated and attributed *History of the Britons* by Nennius appears, and this work is concerned primarily with Celtic legends from centuries earlier. Otherwise, the closest thing we have to a contemporary historical record of the reign of Offa and the 8th century period of Mercian domination are the letters of Alcuin of York, primarily a teacher of theology and a poet. Not only does this correspondence focus on the morality, rather than the detail of contemporary events, but, in the case of English history, Alcuin's writing is often based on second hand accounts, as he spent much of his adult life at the court of Charlemagne in modern Germany, in France and attendant upon the Pope in Rome. As the tutor of both Charlemagne and his sons, Alcuin was respected as the greatest teacher in Europe. As such his correspondence is both startlingly frank and addressed to many of the most important clergy and princes in Europe, including Offa himself. Unfortunately as a consequence, Alcuin often mentions events without describing them, as he assumes his correspondent will know the details himself. His letter to Eardwulf, King of Northumbria, of 796, for example, provides our only reference to a succession crisis that Eardwulf had evidently recently overcome: 'You know very well from what perils the divine mercy has freed you, and how easily it promoted you, when it chose, to the kingship'[168]. Eardwulf may have known from what perils he had been freed. Alas we do not.

After Alcuin, our next great historiographical source is the formidable *Anglo-Saxon Chronicle*, a remarkable yearly record of events, begun in the

---

[167] Bede (2011) p.386
[168] 'Letter of Alcuin to Eardwulf, king of Northumbria' (796, after May) E.H.D. Vol. 1 p. 851

later years of Alfred the Great's reign, circa 990, and continued beyond the Norman Conquest into the 12th century. Uniquely, it seems to have been conceived by Alfred as a national history project, adding literary credence to his vision of a united England under his rule. As a consequence, versions were written and continually updated in monasteries throughout the country, including Canterbury and Peterborough, broadly in agreement with each other, but varying in their inclusion of details. The version we have today is an amalgam of the nine surviving copies plus extracts from later historians who had access to versions of the *Chronicle* now lost to us[169]. The *Chronicles'* monastic authors were anonymous and multiple, and for nearly two centuries they faithfully recorded yearly entries of the events around them they believed to be significant. This section of the *Chronicle* is usually detailed, relatively objective and helpfully precise as to places, names and events. For instance, this is the entry for 890:

'In this year Abbot Beornhelm took to Rome the alms of the West Saxons and of King Alfred. And the northern king, Guthrum, whose baptismal name was Athelstan, died. He was King Alfred's godson, and lived in East Anglia and was the first to settle that land. And in the same year the Danish army went from the Seine to St Lo, which lies between Britanny and France, and the Bretons fought against them and had the victory, and drove them into a river and drowned many of them. In this year Plegmund was elected by God and all the people to the archbishophric of Canterbury'.[170]

By contrast, years before the *Chronicle* was written (it perputes to record them as far back as 1 AD) are much more scanty, of uncertain provenance, and show a lack of interest in events taking place beyond the borders of Wessex. This is particularly problematic for students of Offa and the Mercian period of domination in the 8th century, for whom the Chronicle is our nearest historiographical source. The entry for 758, for instance, simply states:

---

[169] The 12th century Chronicler William of Malmesbury for example preserved a section on the reign of Canute in the early 11th century that would be otherwise unknown to us.
[170] *Anglo-Saxon Chronicle* entry for the Year 890 E.H.D. Vol. 1

'This year Archbishop Cuthbert died.'[171]

Of all the Anglo-Saxon kings, Alfred is the most thoroughly covered by contemporary evidence. Not only are the *Anglo-Saxon Chronicle's* entries comparatively thorough, but we also possess a unique biography by his friend and courtier Asser, Bishop of Sherborne. Both accounts are unashamedly sycophantic, written at the behest of Alfred as part of his wider programme of promoting an English national identity, with himself at its centre as the saviour and rightful ruler of his people. That said, Asser's account is precise in its treatment of the chronology and location of events, and for the first time since Bede, provides an insight into the thought process of an Anglo-Saxon king rather than just his actions, recording, for example, Alfred's regret at his limited education: [He] suffered no greater distress of any kind inwardly and outwardly... and used to moan and sigh continually because Almighty God had created him lacking in divine learning and knowledge of the liberal arts'[172]. Unfortunately, Asser's level of detail is inconsistent, thorough in matters that interested him, such as the king's learning, but scanty in its treatment of such vital events in Alfred's reign as his decisive victory over the Vikings at Edington in 878. This battle, possibly the most import in English history, is largely a mystery to us, dependent as we are on the following description: 'When the next morning dawned he [Alfred] moved his forces and came to a place called Edington and fighting fiercely with a compact shield wall against the entire Viking army, he persevered resolutely for a long time; at length he gained the victory through God's will. He destroyed the Vikings with great slaughter, and pursued those who fled as far as the stronghold' [173].

Our understanding of Alfred's reign is also uniquely enriched by the words of the king himself in the prefaces he writes to his translations of theological and philosophical works. Although not historiography *per se*, these prefaces provide an invaluable insight into the mindset and political agenda of the man who, more than anyone else, created England. The most insightful of

---

[171] Ibid p.177
[172] Asser 76 in Ed. Keynes S. and Lapidge M. (London, 2004) p.92
[173] Ibid 56 p. 84

these is his preface to *Gregory's Pastoral Care* in which he explains the rationale of his revolutionary decision to commission books, not in scholarly Latin, but in the vernacular of Wessex, Old English: 'I recalled how the Law was first composed in the Hebrew language, and thereafter, when the Greeks learned it they translated it into their own language... Therefore it seems better to me... that we too should turn into the language that we can all understand certain books which are the most necessary for men to know'.[174]

Our historiography of the 10th and 11th centuries are ironically scantier than the 9th, owing to the destruction of primary material. The *Anglo-Saxon Chronicle* provides a constant source of reference throughout the period, enriched by the incomplete Aethelweard's *Chronicle*, largely derived from the former, but containing extra material after 892. However, there is no 10th century equivalent of Asser to provide detail of *why* as opposed to how things happened. Our closest detailed references come from the excellent 12th century monastic historians William of Malmesbury and Florence of Worcester, both of whom were pre-eminent historians in their own time and had access to primary documents now lost to us. William of Malmesbury's account of the reign of Alfred's grandson King Athelstan, for instance, is apparently based on an extremely detailed poetic biography William discovered in the library of Malmesbury Abbey, burial place of Athelstan. William does not give the name of the author of the poem, and heavily paraphrases what it said, except for one tantalising extract which he provides on Athelstan's last battle in 939, fought against the Viking King of York Olaf Guthfrithsson: 'He [Athelstan] had passed five and three and four years ruling his subjects by law, subduing tyrants by force, when there returned that plague and hateful ruin of Europe. Now the fierce savagery of the North couches on our land, now the pirate Olaf, deserting the sea, camps in the field, breathing forbidden and savage threats'.[175]

Florence of Worcester evidently had access to similarly detailed

---

[174] Alfred 'Prose preface' to *Translation of Gregory's Pastoral Care* Ibid. p. 126
[175] Cited in William of Malmesbury *Concerning the Acts of the Kings of England* in E.H.D. Vol. 1 p. 303

evidence, from which he compiled his history of the Danish kings of England in the early 11th century. Although, unlike William of Malmesbury, he does not refer to them. By this point, though we have corroboration in the first surviving Viking sagas, praise songs of the deeds of Viking leaders committed to memory by musicians, known as *skalds,* and written down in the 12th and 13th century. Although there are obvious problems with accuracy and exaggeration, when used in corroboration with the strictly chronological and drily objective Florence of Worcester, a detailed picture of the deeds and thinking of King Canute and his followers emerges. The following, for instance, is a dramatic, but believed-to-be accurate recollection of fighting in the Battle of Brunaburgh between Athelstan's English army and that of a Viking led Celtic coalition which potentially contains the first mention of the use of the yew longbow in English warfare: 'The flying javelin bit, peace was broken; the elm-bow was spanned, and the wolf rejoiced at it, The yew bow twanged when swords were drawn'[176].

Between the dry factual chronology of the *Anglo-Saxon Chronicle* and the vivid Norse sagas we have one more piece of pseudo-historiography from the 10th/11th century period, a vivid but geographically and tactically exact poem *The Battle of Maldon*, describing a pyrrhic Viking victory against the *fyrd* of Essex under *Earldoman* Byrthnoth in 991. Whilst it does not add to our understanding of the politics of 991 (Aethelred the Unready reign) contained within the *Anglo-Saxon Chronicle*, it does provide the most detailed and apparently accurate description of the infantry tactics used by both Viking and English in the early medieval period, as well as an excellent insight into the social hierarchy of Anglo-Saxon England. On seeing the death of Brythnoth, his *hearthweru* resolve to stand and fight to the death over the body of their lord, for to retreat would mean breaking their oath of allegiance. One of them, Aelfwine, rallies his comrades as follows:

'Remember the words that we uttered many times over the mead, when on the bench, heroes in the hall, we made our boast about hard strife. Now it

---

[176] Extract from the *Saga of Egil Skala-Grimsson* Ibid. p.324

may be proved which of us is bold... *Thegns* shall have no cause to reproach me among my people that I was ready to forsake this action, and seek my home, now that my lord lies low, cut down in battle. This is no common grief to me, he was both my kinsman and my lord.'[177]

Our only other historiographical accounts of this last phase of Anglo-Saxon England are the detailed, but often flawed German *Chronicle of Theitmar of Merseberg* and the *Encomium Emmae Reginane* from the Abbey of St Omer, France, dealing with Swein Forkbeard, briefly king of England in 1017, and Emma, wife to both Aethelred the Unready and Canute. Both provide useful insights into the attitudes of the individuals they depict, but are clearly flawed in their chronology and comprehension of the facts. After this our next sources are largely Norman, such as William of Poitiers, chaplain to the future William I and the ubiquitous Bayeux Tapestry commissioned by Odo, half-brother of William in the immediate aftermath of the conquest. In all cases, their sole focus is on the events leading up to the conquest of 1066, rather than Anglo-Saxon England *per se*. They do provide some incidental information which we can use retrospectively; the Bayeux Tapestry is our finest source for the equipment of warriors of the late Anglo-Saxon period for instance; but for the most part they look forwards to Norman England and are thus beyond the remit of our survey.

English huscarls fight Norman knights on the Bayeux Tapestry. Details of tactics, armour and weaponry can be derived from this.

---

[177] Anon. *The Battle of Maldon* Ibid. p. 323

Other primary evidence

Our limited supply of historiography on the Anglo-Saxon period means that archaeological remains and finds assume a more central place in early medieval historical research than would be the case in later periods, where the disciplines of history and archaeology often work in isolation. Although our inheritance of Anglo-Saxon documents is frugal, our archaeological record for them is exceptionally rich and enriching further all the time, as the 2003 discovery of a new hoard of gold in Staffordshire from the 7th or 8th century indicates.

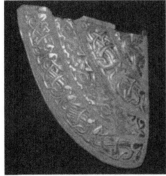

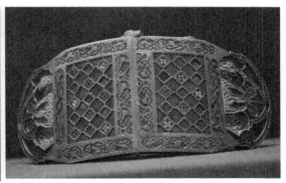

Helmet cheekpiece from the Staffordshire Hoard.

Jewelled shoulder clasp from the Sutton Hoo excavation

The greatest example of Anglo-Saxon archaeology comes from the very start of the period we are assessing – the famous Sutton Hoo ship burial discovered in Suffolk in 1939. Almost certainly the grave of Raedwald, the 6th-7th century East Anglian king and *bretwalda,* who killed the first ruler of a united Northumbria, Aethelfrith in 616, Sutton Hoo has transformed our understanding of the Anglo-Saxon period, perhaps more than any other evidence dispelling the pre-20th century stereotype of a 'Dark Age'. Not only were the metalwork finds of a quality comparable with the best in the 7th century world, goods from as far away as Constantinople provide glimpses into elaborate trading routes, which written records do not mention. Underground finds are not confined to possessions of the mighty, however. Our growing appreciation of the relative wealth of Anglo-Saxon England from the 7th century onwards has been fuelled by extensive finds of coins and luxury items belonging to non-nobles, such as elaborately worked golden broaches found in the graves of wealthy *ceorls* at Lechlade in Gloucestershire, providing evidence of surplus income[178].

Above ground remains also provide valuable evidence, particularly of the sparsely recorded 8th century. Offa's Dyke, the largest archaeological site in Britain, is the ultimate example of this. It is through an appreciation of the complexity of the engineering and workforce challenges involved in creating such a massive fortification that we have developed our understanding of the power and organisation of Mercia under Offa, rather than via the slender record provided by charters, letters and terse entries in the *Anglo-Saxon Chronicle*. Most visible of all are the Anglo-Saxon era's legacy of the vast majority of England's place names. Their evidence is essential in tracking the migration of peoples and the extent of conquests. Although most useful for research into the almost entirely undocumented migration period at the start of the Anglo-Saxon era, place names do assist our understanding of the later era too. The comparatively late emergence of Wessex as a united state in the mid-7th century, compared to Mercia and Northumbria, for instance, was indicated by the persistence of Celtic words in the settlements and geographical features of Devon and Somerset compared to their almost complete disappearance in neighbouring Wiltshire and Dorset. A high piece of ground in the latter is therefore a 'hill'; in the former it is often a 'tor'. [179] Similarly our best indicator for the pattern of Viking settlement in England following the conquests of the 9th century lies in charting the use of Scandinavian suffixes such as –*by* e.g. Whitby. The University of Nottingham's Centre for Name Studies has used this to produce a digital map of Viking conquest that exactly matches Asser and the *Anglo-Saxon Chronicle's* record.[180]

---

[178] These are on display at Corinium Museum, Cirencester.
[179] Coates R. 'Invisible Britons: the view from linguistics' paper presented at conference "Britons in Anglo-Saxon England", organised by Dr Nicholas Higham, Manchester, 14-16 April 2004.
[180] https://www.mysociety.org/2014/04/15/mapping-the-vikings-influence-on-uk-place-names accessed on 20/05/2015

The 'Dark Age' Myth

William of Malmesbury and Florence of Worcester were the exception amongst post-1066 chroniclers in the positive approach they brought to Anglo-Saxon history, both of them being half-English themselves. Architecturally and politically, the new Norman owners of England sought to assert their supremacy through the systematic demolition of what had gone before – today not a single Anglo-Saxon cathedral or abbey remains standing, whilst the introduction of Norman French and the language of court and Latin as the language of learning and governance saw Old English steadily relegated to the status of an oral language divorced from its vibrant literary tradition.

There was less agreement than was once thought amongst the Normans and their chroniclers as to the righteousness of their conquest. However, opposition seems to have been on humanitarian, as opposed to cultural, grounds. A broad consensus amongst post-Conquest chroniclers tended towards the view that the English were a barbaric people in sore need of Norman civilisation.

Odericus Vitalis epitomises this rather confused view. Despite being of Anglo-Norman parentage himself, he was convinced of the need for the conquest, 'England, stained by the cruelties and perjury of Harold Godwinson, fell to decay'. [181] However, as a result of the abuses of their Norman conquerors, the English 'Groaned aloud for their lost liberty and plotted ceaselessly to find some way of shaking off a yoke that was so intolerable and unaccustomed' [182]. There was, however, no state sanctioned policy of re-writing history to barbarianise the English – the Normans were aware that much of their legitimacy lay in their pledges to uphold the ancient laws, traditions and governmental structures of the English state, most of which had its foundations in Alfred the Great and his successors. It seems neglect,

---

[181] Odericus Vitalis *Ecclesiastical History of England and Normandy* Part II Book IV Chapter 2 in E.H.D. Vol. 1.
[182] Ibid. Chapter 4

rather than deliberate intent, was at the heart of an ebbing interest in the study of pre-Conquest England, the progressive disappearance of Old English speakers in the 12th century meaning that, although copies of Bede, Asser and the *Anglo-Saxon Chronicle* remained in monastic libraries, there was nobody to read them. Pre-Norman England thus became a mysterious place, but one which many looked back on fondly as a land of *pristina libertas*, 'pristine liberty', when compared to the perceived oppression of the Norman feudal system. This was particularly apparent in the early 13th century when the signing of Magna Carta by King John created widespread debate about the notion of 'liberty'[183] and resurrected folk memories of English resistance to the Norman conquest – the fenland rebel of the 1060s and 70s. Hereward the Wake's career was intensely charted in Richard of Ely's *Gesta Herewardii* and the subsequent *Register of Robert of Swaffham*, so much so that it may have inspired part of the Robin Hood legend which was set in the reign of King John.

The first promulgator of the 'Dark Age' myth of pre-conquest English savagery was, in fact, not the Norman government at all, but a Welsh poet Geoffrey of Monmouth. Writing in the 1130s, Geoffrey's *History of the Kings of Britain* was allegedly a translation of an ancient Celtic history, but now is regarded largely as a work of fiction whose purpose was to glorify the British ancestors of the Welsh and, in particular, the mythical leader of resistance against the Anglo-Saxons, Arthur. Unsurprisingly, the Anglo-Saxons emerge as the villains of the narrative, as this section on how the legendary 6th century British war leader Vortigern was ambushed indicates:

Modern window of Geoffrey of Monmouth, originator of the 'Dark Age' myth of Anglo-Saxon barbarism.

[183] Crick, J. '*Pristina libertas*: Liberty and the Anglo-Saxons revisited' in *Transactions of the R.H.S.* 14 (2004) pp. 47-71

'Many fell on both sides, but the Saxons got the victory; because the Britons, having no suspicion of treachery, came unarmed, and therefore made a weaker defence. After the commission of this detestable villany, the Saxons would not kill Vortigern; but having threatened him with death and bound him, demanded his cities and fortified places in consideration of their granting him his life. He, to secure himself, denied them nothing; and when they had made him confirm his grants with an oath, they released him from his chains, and then marched first to London, which they took, as they did afterwards York, Lincoln, and Winchester; wasting the countries through which they passed, and destroying the people, as wolves do sheep when left by their shepherds. When Vortigern saw the desolation which they made, he retired into the parts of Cambria, not knowing what to do against so barbarous a people[184].'

So vivid was Geoffrey's prose that it was accepted uncritically throughout Europe into the 16th century and in so doing gave rise to two enduring myths – the Dark Age ignorance and savagery of the Anglo-Saxons and the utopian legend of Arthur and Camelot.

Two further developments perpetuated these legends. The first was the emergence of the humanist tradition of history, beginning with the 14th century Italian Petrarch, which emphasised the greatness of classical learning and the degree to which that learning had been obscured during the period between the fall of Rome in the 6th century and the rise of the renaissance in his own. Anglo-Saxon learning and progress was swept up with that of the Carolingians and the rest of the early medieval into Petrarch's notion of an age of ignorance. Reformation historians subsequently built upon the Dark Age construct further; it suited their theology to portray the early medieval period as a time when the Church corrupted and distorted the true learning of the early Church. As Stuart historian and clergyman, Gilbert Burnet, wrote in 1679 in his *The History of the Reformation of the Church of England*,: "The design of the reformation was to restore Christianity to what it was at first, and to purge it of those corruptions, with which it was overrun in the later and

---

[184] Geoffrey of Monmouth *History of the Kings of Britain* Ch. XVI in E.H.D. Vol. 1

darker age'.[185] The second was the accession in 1485 of the Tudors, a Welsh dynasty with extremely shaky claims to the throne. A mythical descent from King Arthur was thus a propaganda gift, Henry VII even went as far as naming his eldest son after him. One modern scholar has even gone as far as suggesting that the Tudor dynasty claimed a monopoly on presentations of Arthur, hence his absence from the Tudor stage.[186] In such an atmosphere, the construct of the Dark Ages enjoyed a new lease of life and this may in part explain why there was only limited protestation from Tudor scholars about the catastrophic destruction wrought upon medieval libraries during Henry VIII's dissolution of the monasteries.

Rejuvenation and survival

Fortunately, this does not present the complete picture: A second, more positive school of Anglo-Saxon historiography survived the medieval period, one which would provide salvation for innumerable manuscripts in the 16th century. The great legacy of legal codes meant that the Anglo-Saxon legacy was never entirely hidden from view, and even at the height of the Norman period, Edward the Confessor, Alfred and Athelstan continued to be regarded as good kings – their tombs at Westminster Abbey, Winchester Cathedral and Malmesbury Abbey, respectively, continued to be places of reverence until the Reformation.

A landmark was reached in the production of Robert of Gloucester's *Metrical Chronicle* of 1300 which heralded the beginning of a late medieval shift away from the linguistic and cultural apartheid of Norman England. Crucially, this book is written in an evolved version of the Anglo-Saxon language, Middle English, and champions the kingship of Alfred the Great who is contrasted to his contemporary Henry III. This signalled the start of a decisive shift towards cultural conciliation between an English and Norman population, which were, in any case, by the 14th century increasingly

---

[185] Burnet, G. *The History of the Reformation of the Church of England* (1679) Vol. 1 Epistle dedicatory
[186] Kohler R.L. 'Where lies Arthur? The curious absence of the figure of King Arthur from the Early Modern Stage' (M. Litt thesis, 2009).

intermingled. Within a hundred years, English had once again become the language of government, administration and culture. Anglo-Saxon texts were once more accessible and late medieval English historians no longer treat 1066 as a cut off beyond which lay unknown and unknowable history. 15th century chronicler John Rous' *Historum Regnum Angliae,* for instance, takes the form of a moral crusade against the enclosure of common land and draws inspiration from no less a patron of humanity than Aethelflaed, daughter of Alfred the Great and *de facto* Queen of Mercia.

This tradition of Anglo-Saxon scholarship persisted into the 16th century, where it ran alongside the Tudor Arthurian tradition. John Leland, who held the unique role of King's Antiquiter in the 1530s, set a precedent for a new, post-monastic tradition of secular history. Fluent in both Welsh and Old English, Leland began a tradition of collecting manuscripts from the early medieval period that was built upon by Robert Talbot in Norwich and the Welshman Robert Recorde, both of whom saved copies of key works, including Bede and the *Anglo-Saxon Chronicle*. These men regarded themselves not as moralistic chroniclers in the medieval tradition, but as antiquarians – collectors of the knowledge of the past for its own sake. By the reign of Elizabeth I in 1558, a circle of Anglo-Saxon antiquarians had formed around the august figure of Matthew Parker, Archbishop of Canterbury. Under his auspices, they scoured remnants of monastic libraries, cathedral archives, private collections and forgotten government offices for manuscripts. Amongst others, they located the sole surviving copies of both *Beowulf* and Asser during this hunt.

By the 1560s the first printed versions of Anglo-Saxon texts were appearing. In 1563, the most successful author of the Elizabethan period, John Foxe, publically declared in his *Book of Martyrs* the need to preserve Old English manuscripts as a means of countering Catholic innovation of religion which, in the absence of records to the contrary 'new thynges were

John Foxe, Elizabethan matyrologist and unlikely champion of Anglo-Saxon historiography.

reported for old'[187]. The body of material available to us today is largely that bequeathed by Parker and his contemporaries. By the slimmest of margins, Anglo-Saxon historiography had survived the Reformation.

Politicisation

The advent of the Stuart dynasty in the 17th century saw Anglo-Saxon historiography thrust to the forefront of political debate for the first time since the 11th century. Contemporary debates as to the relative power of monarchy and parliament, which ultimately erupted into the British civil wars of the 1640s and 50s, were fuelled by a growing awareness of Anglo-Saxon history, the legacy of which was used by both sides: The royalist interpretation of Richard Verstagen[188] emphasised the line of descent between the Wessex dynasty and the contemporary Stuarts as a means of reinforcing their legitimacy, whilst no less an individual than John Milton countered with reference to a golden age of English freedom before the Norman Conquest, directly equating the Stuart King Charles I's attempts to retain Parliament with 'the yoke of an outlandish conqueror[189]' laid upon Anglo-Saxon England by William the Conqueror. In particular, the institution of Parliament was erroneously portrayed as having descended from Anglo-Saxon *witans* and *moots*.

---

[187] Foxe J. *Book of Martyrs* (1563)
[188] Verstagen R. *Restitution of Decayed intelligence in Antiquities* (1605)
[189] Milton J. *The History of Britain* (1670) Book 6

John Milton, poet, avid Parliamentarian and perpetuator of the myth of Anglo-Saxon 'pristine liberty'.

The notion of the Anglo-Saxons as early architects of liberty was picked up by the Whig school of history which dominated 18th and early 19th century scholarship. Viewing human history as a steadily developing evolution of mankind from a condition of tyranny to liberty, Whiggism was inevitably attracted to the myth of pre-Conquest parliamentary tradition. The Germanic origins of the reigning Hanoverian dynasty made political references to the Germanic Anglo-Saxons politically desirable too, particularly as the basis of that dynasty's seizure of the throne off the Stuarts was that they would uphold the 'ancient freedoms' of the English people and their parliament.

Alfred the Great, in particular, was promoted as a role model of enlightened kingship both by historians [190] and in popular culture. Indeed, during this period, an epidemic of monument building took place at sites associated with him, including the Alfred Tower on the Stourhead estate in Wiltshire, on the supposed site of Egbert's Stone where the king rallied his troops prior

Role model of enlightened kingship - Alfred the Great's bust from the Temple of the Worthies, an 18th century folly at Stowe House, Buckinghamshire.

---

[190] The most influential was Paul de Rapin Thomas' *The History*

to the Battle of Edington in 878. The inscription on this tower effectively summarises the 18th century cult of enlightened kingship which had grown up around Alfred:

'Alfred The Light of a Benighted Age
Was a philosopher and a Christian
The Father of his People
The Founder of the English Monarchy and
liberty.[191]

The Victorians took this idealisation of Anglo-Saxon virtue further in the age of Empire, adding a sinister racial overtone. Seeking to explain and justify Britain's rising imperial power across the world, historians such as John Mitchell Kemble emphasised the uniqueness of English institutions and English character, arguing that both of these originated in the unique Germanic civilisation of the Anglo-Saxons, which featured 'a love of freedom and a hatred of anarchic disorder coupled with a respect for the law... to be able to exhibit restraint, self-control, rational thinking and have a healthy distrust for enthusiasm'[192]. Quasi-scientific research following the 19th century fad for eugenics attempted to root these qualities in biological terms – the fact that the following was published in the Royal Historical Society's journal in 1885 indicates how far notions of racial hierarchy had penetrated the academic establishment of late Victorian Britain:

'Of our mental qualities we appear to derive from the Saxon our practical common sense, our business capacity, and our power of adapting ourselves to circumstances, and what we may call in general terms, the faculty of colonisation'[193].

---

[191] Words attributed to the banker and amateur historian Henry Hoare (1705-80) who built the Stourhead estate in the 1760s.
[192] Hill P. *The Anglo-Saxons: The Verdict of History* (Stroud, 2006) pp. 153-54
[193] Foster Palmer J. 'The Saxon Invasion and its influence on our Character as a race' in *Transactions of the Royal Historical Society* Vol. 2 Issue 2. June 1885 pp. 173-96

Such beliefs coincided, and contributed to, the emergence of the Anglo-Saxons as a mainstream cultural staple. Dedicated chairs of Anglo-Saxon history were established at the newly established 'red brick universities', fanciful monuments and paintings abounded in public and private institutions[194] and even Anglo-Saxon Christian names, such as Cedric and Athelstan, enjoyed a renaissance. This fashion reached a climax in 1899 with a millennial commemoration of Alfred the Great's death, centred on his capital of Winchester – the city corporation commissioned a 15 foot high bronze statue which dominates the approach to the town hall by Britain's leading sculptor Sir Hamo Thorneycroft .

Alfred the Great's statue in Winchester – the ultimate expression of Victorian fondness for the Anglo-Saxons.

20th century controversy

The rise of Germanophobia and the concurrent results of the World Wars severely dented the cultural reputation of the Germanic Anglo-Saxons – the Victorian notions of cultural and racial supremacy were deeply unfashionable in the aftermath of World War Two. Early 20th century historians, such as FW Maitland[195], began to swing back in favour of the Normans as the founder of the modern British state.

Archaeology was, however, to come to the assistance of Anglo-Saxon history. The remarkable discovery of the Sutton Hoo burial ship in 1939 provided physical evidence which conclusively dealt with the 'Dark Age' myth of Anglo-Saxon barbarism.

---

[194] The Palace of Westminster, rebuilt after a disastrous fire in the 1840s, features over 20 paintings and sculptures from the Anglo-Saxon period including three on Alfred and no less than 11 on the conversion of the English to Christianity.
[195] Maitland (1897)

Elsewhere three interwar academics ensured the survival of Anglo-Saxon history as a discipline. Historians Sir Frank Stenton and Dorothy Whitelock produced definitive political and cultural histories, as well as a standardised compilation of contemporary documents, whilst JRR Tolkien revamped Anglo-Saxon language and literature – producing definitive dictionaries of early English, a new vibrant translation of Beowulf and most famously his *Hobbit* and *Lord of the Rings* novels whose fantasy world has given Anglo-Saxon culture its most accessible face.

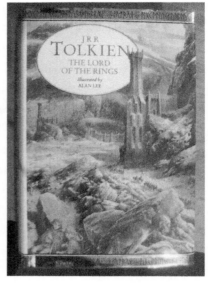

The accessible face of Anglo-Saxon England – JRR Tolkein's *Lord of the Rings*.

Current thought

Anglo-Saxon history continues to be neglected in Britain. At a school level, the artificial cut off between pre- and post- 1066 which occurs between the last year of primary and the first year of secondary education has resulted in an ongoing artificial separation between early medieval and the rest of British history. At university it, along with the rest of the medieval period, suffers from the current obsession with modern and Tudor history. What it lacks in mass engagement it makes up for in quality, however, and the historiography of the last fifty years has been vibrant and well informed.

The very limited pool of evidence bequeathed to us defines the limits of Anglo-Saxon historiography in a manner more familiar to students of classics than those of more modern periods, when the reverse problem tends to apply. As a result, studies of Alfred the Great and the last years of the period from the reign of Aethelred the Unready onwards have tended to predominate, as these are the most richly endowed with primary sources.

Scarcity has in recent years given rise to increasing ingenuity, however, making substantial surveys of what were formerly shadowy figures, hitherto known largely through the brief entries of the *Anglo-Saxon Chronicle*. In part, this is the consequence of the rise of 'study centres', interdisciplinary academic bodies combining historical, archaeological, theological, linguistic, scientific and literary methods to make links and conclusions in a manner that would have been inconceivable a generation earlier. Some of these are broad in their remit, capable of assessing trends across centuries and millennia, such as the University of Bristol centre for medieval studies. Others are specific and localised, such as the Bernician Studies Group, whose work made possible the first work of popular history on the 7th century, Max Adams' biography of Oswald of Northumbria[196], hitherto squarely rooted in 'Dark Age' mystery.

Moreover, the modern biographical technique known as 'structuration', which seeks to understand the contribution of a person by establishing a dialectic between the beliefs and actions of an individual and the deep structures of the society and state they operate in working reciprocally, has enabled us to examine the motivations as opposed to the simple actions of individuals. Sarah Foot's biography of Athelstan[197] is the definitive academic example of this, whilst popular historian Michael Wood has used this technique to impressive effect in an archeologically led approach, most recently on Alfred the Great's daughter Aethelflaed 'Lady of the Mercians'[198].

More broadly, historiography of the era has increasingly assessed long term trends within the Anglo-Saxon period within a broader narrative which tends towards emphasising continuity between this and the periods before and after. The origins of the English nation state is the definitive area of research in this field. The traditional cut-off of 1066 as the moment the English

---

[196] Adams M *The King in the North: The life and times of Oswald of Northumbria* (London, 2013)
[197] Foot (2011)
[198] Wood M 'The Lady of the Mercians' first transmitted on BBC Four 22.08.14

nation state came into being was voiced by Stenton in the early 20th century. However, by the end of his career, he was antedating many of its institutions to the pre-Conquest period. Modern scholarship goes further, arguing not only that Anglo-Saxon England was a nation state, but that it was *the* first nation state: 'It may seem extravagant to describe early England as a 'nation-state'. Nevertheless it is unavoidable.' [199]

Further Reading:

A. Gransden, *Historical Writing in England c. 550–1307* (Routledge, London 1974)

P. Hill *Anglo-Saxons: The Verdict of History* (The History Press, Stroud 2006)

Questions to consider

- Given the limitations of the evidence, is it possible to write objective history about the Anglo-Saxons?

- To what extent has the history of Anglo-Saxon England been used as a weapon in contemporary political battles?

- 'Irrelevant to the modern age'. Discuss this view of Anglo-Saxon historiography.

---

[199] Campbell J 'The united kingdom of England: the Anglo-Saxon achievement' in Ed. Grant A. and Strigner KJ. *Uniting the Kingdom: The making of English History* (London, 1995) p.31. David Starkey makes the case for England being the first country to undergo the process of nation state making in Starkey (2004) p. 69

Glossary

Note: The spoken language of the English throughout the early medieval period was what we know call Old English, a distant ancestor of the modern language, possessing many of the same words and mostly the same sentence structure, although it did use masculine and feminine tenses which fell out of favour during the transition to Middle English in the aftermath of the Norman Conquest. Before the reign of Alfred the Great (871-899) Old English was almost entirely an aural language; the language of scholarship and writing being Latin. It was Alfred who commanded that Old English be the language of government, scholarship and literature, as part of his programme of nation building. Inevitably, a large number of Scandinavian words crept into the common use as a result of the Viking settlements from the mid-9th century onwards. In this book Old English, Latin and Scandinavian words are used where there is no modern English equivalent.

AENGLA LAND: The original spelling of 'England', literally 'Land of the Angles. This became the accepted word for the united kingdom of the English people in the 10th century.

AETHLING: 'Heir', usually to a crown. More than one *aethling* could exist, nominated either by the reigning king or the senior nobility. *Aethlings* were not guaranteed to inherit the throne, the word simply implied that they were a contender.

ANGELCYNN: The English people, a term loaded with political significance by Alfred the Great and his successors.

ANGLES: One of the Germanic tribes that invaded England from the 5th century onwards. Orginally from Angelm in modern day north Germany, they settled in Northumbria, East Anglia and eastern Mercia. The words 'English' and 'England' are derived from them.

BONDSMAN: An umbrella term for an individual legally belonging to another in medieval Europe. After the Norman Conquest the majority of English people fell under this status.

BOOKLAND: Land gifted to the Church for all eternity. It was normally exempt from taxation.

BRETWALDA: Literally 'Britain-ruler', an honorific the historian Bede gave to particularly powerful Anglo-Saxon kings.

BURGH/BOROUGH: A fortified, self-governing town used by the Cerdicynn dynasty and the Danes as centres of government and warfare.

BYZANTINE: The eastern, Greek speaking half of the Roman Empire that survived into the 15th century. For much of the early medieval period it was the greatest power in eastern Europe.

CALIPHATE: A form of Islamic emperor whose authority was based on claimed descent from the Prophet Mohammed.

CANONISATION: The process whereby the Pope declares an individual a saint.

CAROLINGIAN: European imperial dynasty founded by Charlemagne (Charles the Great) who reigned 800-814.

CATHOLIC: The part of Christendom obedient to the Pope.

CEORL: A free peasant farmer in Anglo-Saxon England liable to taxation and service in the *fyrd*.

CERDICYNN: The royal dynasty of Wessex claiming descent from Cerdic, a Saxon chieftain who was supposedly first King of Wessex 519-34. Cerdic was a pagan who claimed descent from the Anglo-Saxon father god, Woden. From the reign of Alfred onwards they became the first rulers of a united England.

CHARTER: A grant of authority or rights, in this case usually property gifted by the king.

CHRISTENDOM: Places under Christian government. During the Anglo-Saxon period Christendom was sandwiched between Moslem lands, in the south, and surviving areas of paganism, in the north and east.

CHURCH: The institutions of Catholic Christianity, the only multi-national organisation in medieval Europe including parish churches, minsters, monasteries, cathedrals, the clergy and their servants. A vast landowner, the guardian of learning and provider of literate staff for government administration, it also administered its own law known as canon law.

CYNEHELM: The royal helmet of kingship, used in place of a crown by Anglo-Saxon kings until the 10th century, reflecting their primary function as leaders of their people in war. A remarkable surviving example was discovered in 1939 at the Sutton Hoo burial site, Suffolk.

DANEGELD: Money extorted from the English by the Vikings as the price for ceasing pillage.

DANELAW: The area of Britain under Viking rule.

DARK AGES: The traditional, pejorative term for the period in Europe, beginning with the fall of the Roman Empire in the 5th and 6th century to the advent of feudalism in the 11th. Most modern historians prefer the more neutral term 'early medieval'.

DOOM: The Old English word for 'judgement'; it has none of the sinister connotations it possesses in modern English.

EARLDOMAN: The senior rank of nobleman in Anglo-Saxon England, typically responsible for a shire. The later title of 'earl' is derived from it.

ECCLESIASTICAL: Matters pertaining to the Church.

EUGENICS: A now discredited branch of science which sought to divide humanity into races which were supposedly engaged in a struggle for survival.

FEUDAL: A combination of legal, military and social customs developed by the Carolingian empire and its successors based on possession of land in return for military service. Its adoption from the 9th century onwards marks the end of the early medieval period.

FOLKLAND: The normal method of landholding in Anglo-Saxon England in which a tenant was granted a lifetime lease of land.

FOLKMOOT: An institution of consultative government, most commonly found in Wessex. The population of a particular shire would gather at an open air meeting place yearly. The king and his *ealdormen* would hear their grievances and make judgements.

FREEMAN: Non-noble individuals who were not owned by anyone. In England the term for a freedman was a *ceorl*.

FYRD: The Anglo-Saxon militia system which required freemen to give temporary military service when required by their king.

GESITH: 'Companions' of the king, a term principally used in the early Anglo-Saxon period to describe the warriors who guarded the royal household. The term was largely replaced by *hearthweru* by the 9th century.

HAGIOGRAPHY: A biography of a saint. These were very popular in Anglo-Saxon England where saints were revered as role models.

HISTORIOGRAPHY: The body of history written about a particular period or individual.

HEARTHWERU: Literally 'hearth warriors', the professional soldiers of Anglo-Saxon England attached to the households of kings and nobles. They formed the core of the army around which the *fyrd* was formed. In the 11th century they were renamed *huscarls*.

HEPTARCHY: A collective term used from the 16th century to describe the seven English kingdoms which emerged by 600 AD – Northumbria, Mercia, Wessex, East Anglia, Essex, Kent and Sussex.

HIDE: A unit of land area roughly equal to that needed to support a peasant household. It formed the basis of taxation and local government.

HOLY ROMAN EMPIRE: A huge central European empire founded by Charlemagne in 800 AD, who claimed to be both the successor to the Roman Empire and guardian of Christianity hence 'Holy Roman.'

HUNDRED: The standard sub-unit of local government in Wessex and latterly south and central England. It roughly contained a hundred families.

HUNDREDMAN: The official responsible for local justice and tax raising in a Hundred. He reported to the *Earldoman* of the shire.

ICLINGAS: The kings of Mercia descended from Icel, an Angle chieftain who in turn claimed descent from the legendary Offa of Angelm, supposedly a descendent of Woden. They reached their zenith under Aethelbald and Offa in the 8th century.

IDINGS: The descendants of Ida (died 559), king of the small north eastern English kingdom of Bernicia who created and ruled over Northumbria, the first coherent English state.

IMPERIUM: The authority of the Roman Emperors often claimed by the most powerful kings of the heptarchy when seeking overlordship over their rivals.

JARL: A Viking aristocrat, loosely the equivalent of *earldoman*.

JUTES: One of the Germanic tribes that invaded England from the 5th century onwards. Originally from Jutland in modern day Denmark, they founded the heptarchic kingdom of Kent.

KULTURKAMPF: Literally 'cultural struggle', a 19th century German term borrowed by historians of the early medieval period to describe the policy of English nation building followed by Alfred and his successors from the late 9th to the late 10th centuries.

LAITY: A term used by the clergy to describe the rest of the population.

LEGATINE: A council or mission led by the Pope's representative, the papal legate.

LITURGY: The officially sanctioned form of Christian worship.

MANCIPIA: The Roman institution of bondsmanship out of which the medieval version was derived.

MANCUSES: A unit of gold currency worth approximately 30 silver pennies.

MAUSOLEUM: A building housing a tomb.

MEDIEVAL: The 'middle period' of European history between Antiquity and the Modern covering approximately 500-1500 AD.

MIMESIS: 'Imitation', a wide ranging philosophical term. In this context it refers to the medieval tradition of learning which sought to gain wisdom through imitating God.

MIGRATION PERIOD: The period immediately following the fall of the Roman Empire characterised by multiple invasions across western Europe, including the influx of the Angles, Saxons and Jutes into Britain from the late 4th century to the end of the 6th century AD.

MINSTER: Large churches established as the centre of Christian missions in England.

MOOT: See *witangameot*.

NATION STATE: A culturally linked people inhabiting a geographically defined area under common government.

ORDINANCE: An order or decree, usually relating to law in Anglo-Saxon England.

ORTHODOX: The Eastern Christian church based in the Byzantine Empire.

PRAEFECTI: The governors of Roman provinces. Their apparatus of local government was often adopted by the early medieval monarchies who succeeded the Roman Empire.

PRETERISTS: An apocalyptic school of Christianity which believed that the world was imminently coming to an end with the Second Coming of Christ.

PRIMOGENITURE: The law of succession whereby the eldest son automatically inherited the throne. The Anglo-Saxons did not use this system, preferring to select the next king from a number of potential heirs or *aethlings*.

PRISTINA LIBERTAS: 'Pristine liberty' – an idealised view of Anglo-Saxon freedom exploited in several political controversies from the 13th century onwards including the signing of Magna Carta in 1215 and the English Civil Wars of 1642-48.

PROVINCIAE: The provinces of the Roman Empire, often retained as the basis of early medieval kingdoms.

RECONQUISTA: The Christian counterattack against the Moslem invaders of Spain, beginning in 718 and completed in 1492.

RENAISSANCE: 'Rebirth', a term coined by 14th century poet Petrarch to describe the rediscovery of learning from classical sources. Historians now use the term to describe earlier periods of renewal in learning, such as that occurring in 6th century Northumbria and late 9th century Wessex.

RING-GIVER: A traditional title of Anglo-Saxon kings signifying the power of patronage, specifically their obligation to reward their followers with rings of gold and silver.

SCEATTA: The first English coin, minted by the kings of Northumbria and Kent from the 680s.

SCIR: A province of the Northumbrian kingdom, forerunner of the shire system.

SCHISM: A divide, usually between components of the Church.

SHIRE: A province of Wessex, following the unification of England by the Cerdicynns the whole country was 'shired'. Later known as counties, they remain the most important unit of local government in England to the present.

SHIRE MAN: The chief judge of a shire.

SHIRE REEVE: The formal title of the *ealdorman* responsible for the governance of a shire, the title metamorphosed into 'sheriff' after the Norman Conquest.

SYNOD: A gathering of clergy.

THEGN: A junior nobleman in Anglo-Saxon England.

TRELLEBORG: A combined fortress and training centre for the standing Danish army created in the late 10th century.

VERNACULAR: The language of the people.

VIR: A fortified hall, the basis of government during the early Anglo-Saxon period.

WAPENTAKE: A sub-division of a shire in the north of England, equivalent of a hundred elsewhere.

WEREGILD: Compensation money paid out to the victims of crime in Anglo-Saxon England.

WITANGAMEOT: The council of nobles in Wessex and from the 10th century onwards England.

ZOOMORPH: Art based on stylised animals.

Bibliography

Primary Documents

(* denotes derived from Ed. Whitelock D *English Historical Documents Vol. I* (London, 1979)

Attrib. Aethelwold *An Old English account of King Edgar's establishment of monasteries* (975-984)*

Letter of Alcuin to Eardwulf, king of Northumbria (796, after May) *

Letter of Alcuin to Offa (787-796) *

Anon. *The Battle of Maldon**

Grant by King Athelstan of Amounderness to the church of York (7 June 934) no. 104*

'Bede's Letter to Egbert' in Ed. McClure J and Collins R, Bede *The Ecclesiastical History of the English People* (c.735) (Oxford, 2008)

Boniface Writes A Letter of Admonition to King Aethelbald of Mercia (746-7) in legacy.fordham.edu/halsall/basis/Boniface-letters.asp

Letter of Boniface to Hwaetberht, Abbot of Wearmouth (746-7)*

Will of King Eadred (951-55)*

Grant by King Eadwig of Southwell to Oscetel, Archbsihop of York (956)*

Grant by King Edgar of land at Kineton, Warwickshire to his thegn Aelfwold (969)

King Edgar's law code at Andover (II and III Edgar 959-63)*

King Edgar's law code issued at "Wihtbordesstan" (IV Edgar 962-3)*

Edmund's code concerning the blood feud (II Edmund 939-946)*

Renewal by King Ethelred for the monastery of St Frideswide, Oxford of a privilege for their Charter No: 127

The Laws of Ine No.32*

Letter of Pope Paul I to Eadberht, King of Northumbria, and his brother Egbert, Archbishop of York (757-8)*

Roger of Wendover 'Treaty Between Charlemagne & Offa' (790) from http://legacy.fordham.edu/halsall/source/790charles-offa.asp accessed on 24/06/15

Charter to Uhtred, sub-king of the Hwicce to Athelmund, son of Ingild, of land at Aston Fields, Stoke Prior, Worcester (770) No. 74*

Primary Historiography

(*denotes derived from Ed. Whitelock D *English Historical Documents Vol. I* (London, 1979)

Abbo of Fleury *Passio Sancti Eadmundi*

Adomnán *Life of St Columba*

Attrib. Aldfrith trans. Ireland, Colin *Briathra Flainn Fhina Maic Ossu*

Alfred, 'Preface to his translation of Augustine's *Soliloques'* in Ed. Keynes S. and Lapidge M. *Asser's Life of Alfred and other Contemporary Sources* (London, 2004)

Alfred 'Prose preface' to *Translation of Gregory's Pastoral Care* in Ed. Keynes S. and Lapidge M. *Asser's Life of Alfred and other Contemporary Sources* (London, 2004)

Anon. *The Anglo-Saxon Chronicle**

Anon. *Beowulf*

Anon. *Life of St Dunstan**

Anon. *Saga of Egil Skala-Grimsson**

Anon. *Encomium Emmae Reginae*

Anon *Life of St Oswald, Archbishop of York* *

Asser 'Life of King Alfred' in Ed. Keynes S and Lapidge M Asser's *Life of Alfred and other Contemporary Sources* (London, 2004)

St Augustine of Hippo *The City of God*

Bede *Life of St Cuthbert*

Bede *Ecclesiastical History of the English Nation*

Burnet, G *The History of the Reformation of the Church of England* (1679)

Foster Palmer J 'The Saxon Invasion and its influence on our Character as a race' in *Transactions of the Royal Historical Society* Vol. 2 Issue 2. June 1885

Floddard's *Annals**

Foxe J *Book of Martyrs*

Geoffrey of Monmouth *History of the Kings of Britain*

Gildas *On the Ruin and Conquest of Britain**

John of Wallingford *The Chronicle*

Milton J *The History of Britain* (1670)

The Chronicle of Regino, Abbot of Prum

Saxo Grammaticus *Gesta Danorum*

Simeon of Durham *History of the kings**

Thietmar of Merseburg *Chronicle**

William of Malmesbury *Gestis Regum Anglorum**

de Rapin Thomas, P *The History of England* (1726)

Verstagen R *Restitution of Decayed intelligence in Antiquities* (1605)

Vitalis, O *Ecclesiastical History of England and Normandy*

Historiography

Abels R. *Alfred the Great: War, Kingship and Culture in Anglo-Saxon England* (Harlow, 1998)

Abernethy S. thefreelancehistorywriter.com accessed on 10/06/2015

Adams M. *The King in the North: The life and times of Oswald of Northumbria* (London, 2013)

Brown M.P. and Farr CA. *Mercia: An Anglo-Saxon Kingdom in Europe* (Leicester University Press 2001)

Brown M.B. *Manuscripts from the Anglo-Saxon Age* (London, 2007)

Crick, J. 'Pristina libertas: Liberty and the Anglo-Saxons revisited' in *Transactions of the R.H.S.* 14 (London, 2004)

Carlyton-Britton P.W.P. 'The Gold Mancus of Offa, King of Mercia' in *British Numismatic Journal* (London, 1908) Vol. 5 No. 5

Davies W and Vierck H, 'The Contexts of Tribal Hidage: Social Aggregates and Settlement Patterns' in *Frühmittelalterliche Studien* 8, (Berlin,1974)

Downham C. *Viking Kings of Britain and Ireland: The Dynasty of Ívarr to A.D. 1014* (Edinburgh, 2007)

Elton M 'Interview with Dr Janina Ramirez' in *BBC History Magazine* August 2015

Foote P. and Wilson D. *The Viking Achievement* (1974, London)

Foot S. *Athelstan: The First King of England* (Yale University Press 2011)

Friends of Malmesbury Abbey *Athelstan: The First King of all England?* (Malmesbury, 2013)

Gransden A. *Historical Writing in England c. 550–1307* (London, 1974)

Hadley D. *The Vikings in England: Settlement, Society and Culture* (Manchester University Press, 2007)

Hasting A. *The Construction of Nationhood: Ethnicity, Religion and Nationalism* (Cambridge University Press, 1997)

Herlihy, David "Demography", in Ed. Strayer, Joseph R., *Dictionary of the Middle Ages* (New York, 1989).

Hill P. *The Anglo-Saxons: The Verdict of History* (Stroud, 2006)

Higham N.J. *The Kingdom of Northumbria AD 350–1100* (Stroud, 1993)

Hodge A. and Quennell P. Editorial: 'When did it become impossible to know everything?' in *History Today* April 1952

Holdsworth P. 'Saxon Southampton; a New Review' in *Southampton Archaeological Research Committee* (Southampton, 1975)

Horspool D. *Alfred the Great* (Stroud, 2014)

Humble R. *The Saxon Kings* (London, 1980)

John E. 'The Return of the Vikings' in Ed Campbell J. *The Anglo-Saxons* (London, 1991)

Jones G. *A History of the Vikings* (London, 1975)

Jury L. 'For the cradle of English civilization go to the Wirral' in *The Independent* 8/12/04

Keynes S. and Lapidge M. 'Notes on Asser's Life of King Alfred' in Ed. Keynes S. and Lapidge M. Asser's *Life of Alfred and other Contemporary Sources* (London, 2004)

Loyn H.R. *The Vikings in Britain* (Tiptree, 1977)

Kohler R.L. 'Where lies Arthur? The curious absence of the figure of King Arthur from the Early Modern Stage' Bachelor of Science thesis in Theatre Arts, Radford University, (2007)

Karkov C. 'The frontispiece to the New minster Charter and the King's Two Bodies' in Ed. Scragg D. *Edgar: King of the English* (Woodbridge, 2008)

Kirby D.P. *The Earliest English Kings* (London, 1991)

Lyon C.S.S. 'A reappraisal of the *seatta* and the *styca* coinage of Northumbria' in *The British Numismatic Journal* (1955) Vol. 28 No. 16

Maitland F.W. *Domesday Book and Beyond* (Cambridge University Press, 1897)

McClure J. and Collins R. 'Explanatory Notes' in Ed. McClure J and Collins R *Bede's Ecclesiastical History* (Oxford, 2008)

Pagan H. 'The Pre-Reform Coinage of Edgar' in Ed. Scragg D *Edgar: King of the English* (Woodbridge, 2008)

Peddie J. *Alfred: Warrior King* (Stroud, 1999)

Pollard J. *Alfred the Great: The Man who made England* (London, 2005)

Pratt D. *The Political Thought of King Alfred the Great* (Cambridge University Press, 2008)

Reynolds S. *Kingdoms and Communities in Western Europe, 900-1300* (Oxford University Press, 1997)

Richard J. *Viking Age England* (Bath, 1991)

Riche P. *The Carolingians: A Family who forged Europe* (University of Pennsylvania Press, 1983)

Rollason D. *Northumbria, 500–1100: Creation and Destruction of a Kingdom* (Cambridge University Press, 2003)

Southern R.W. *The Making of the Middle Ages* (Yale University Press, 1973)

Starkey D. *The Monarchy of England Volume 1: Beginnings* (London, 2004)

Stenton F.M. *Anglo-Saxon England* (Oxford University Press, 1987)

Stubbs W. *The Constitutional History of England: Its Origins and Development* (Cambridge University Press, 1903)

Ed. Vaughan R. and Hudson B. *Viking Pirates and Christian Princes: Dynasty, Religion and Empire in the North Atlantic* (Oxford University Press 2007)

Williams A. *Aethelred the Unready – The ill-counselled king* (London, 2003)

Wood M. *In search of the Dark Ages* (London, 2003)

Wood M. *Alfred the Great and the Anglo-Saxons* (BBC television series first broadcast 2014)

Wood M. 'The Lady of the Mercians' first transmitted on BBC Four 22.08.14

Yorke, B. "Alfred the Great: The most perfect man in history?" in *History Today* Vol. 49 Issue 10 Nov. 1999